Thai Vegetarian Cooking

Thai Vegetarian Cooking

SD BOOKS
A Trademark of Sangdad Publishing

Thai Vegetarian Cooking

ISBN 978-974-05-8934-1
First Published October 2008 by
Sangdad Publishing Co., Ltd.
Price 790 Baht

Text & Photography Copyright © 2008 by
Sangdad Publishing Co., Ltd.

Director Thavithong Hongvivatana **Managing Director** Nidda Hongwiwat
Vice Managing Director Jiranan Tubniem **General Manager** Nan Hongvivatana
Production Director Jiranan Tubniem **Marketing Director** Pranee Pongpun
Editor-in-Chief Nan Hongvivatana **Food Editor** Obchoel Imsabai
Recipe Consultant Khanruk Nawaboonniyom **English Editor** Oranuch Wangsuekul
Editor Nidda Hongwiwat **Coordinator** Oeung-arin Saichan
Editorial Staff Yaowapa Kwandussadee, Sirilak Rodyan, Buppha Kittikul
Art Director Samart Sudto **Assistant Art Director** Bhinnasak Kaewyai **Layout** Narumon Thongbai
Photography Sangdad Studio **Slides Bank** Thongpoon Malasri, Aroonluk Puenpinij, Pranom Krongsee
Proof Reader Oeung-arin Saichan **Marketing** Boonjarean Muansri, Chatchai Kangman, Apiruk Meepaw, Nong Pusomsri **Finance** Chonticha Uamduang, Wannee Hoychote, Maliwan Jenjobe
Production Napakan Khumchaiyapoom, Yuttachai Pimsalee, Kanokwan Sonsukon
Color Separation Scan Art Co., Ltd. Tel. (66) 2292-0279-81
Printer Pimdee Co., Ltd. Tel. (66) 2803-2694-7

Publisher and Distributor Sangdad Publishing Co., Ltd.
320 Lad Phrao 94 (Town in Town), Wangthonglang, Bangkok 10310, Thailand
Tel. (66) 2934-4413 ext. 102-110 Fax. (66) 2538-1499, (66) 2934-4415
E-mail: marketing@sangdad.com **www.sangdad.com**

Contents

Spicy Dips

Curries

Stir-Fried and Fried

Contents

Introduction

Traditionally Thai people ate a vegetable-based diet with fair amount of fresh-water fishes and poultry. That is to say in the old days the majority of Thais, who are Buddhists, were naturally *demi-vegan*. However, as the country becomes more affluent and its cuisine developed and differentiated, meat, particularly pork and poultry, plays more and more important role in Thai cooking. Vegetarianism had been confined mainly to the Chinese Buddhist temples and devoted Thai-Chinese populations. Fortunately since the advent of Santi Asoke Sect advocating vegetarianism as an essential Buddhist precept about 30 years ago, Thai vegetarian cooking has been increasingly gaining momentum.

In a nut shell, Thai vegetarian cooking is simply the use of non-meat ingredients in Thai cuisine which is characterized by hot, pungent and aromatic flavors. Yet due to influence of Chinese and lately other Southeast Asian cuisines as well, a number of Thai vegetarian dishes have mild flavors. Therefore, in this book of Thai Vegetarian Cooking, there are quite a lot of recipe choices to choose from.

Soy Products

The art of Thai vegetarian cooking centers around the use of soy products to substitute meat. This applies also to vegetarian shrimp paste which is simply the substitution of fermented soy bean for shrimps and seasoned to approximate the taste of real shrimp paste. Vegetarian fermented fish was produced in the same fashion. Yet vegetarian oyster sauce is another case where shiitake mushroom is used in place of oyster.

Soft tofu

Hard tofu

Important soy products for meat substitution in Thai vegetarian cooking are the following.

Tofu There are two basic types – soft and hard. *Soft or silk tofu* is best for soup. It could as well appropriate for steaming and stir-fry, or even mashed to a tasty dip. With firm texture, *hard tofu* could be boiled, steamed, roasted, fried, and even grilled. It is ideal ingredient to replace meat in most dishes. Soft and hard tofu can be further cooked to make turmeric yellow-skin tofu and soy sauce black-skin tofu. The firm yellow-skin tofu is used in the famous *Phad Thai* noodle. *Tube tofu* is just soft tofu in plastic tube. *Tofu string or tofu ring* is simply several small firm tofu fried to golden brown and puffy.

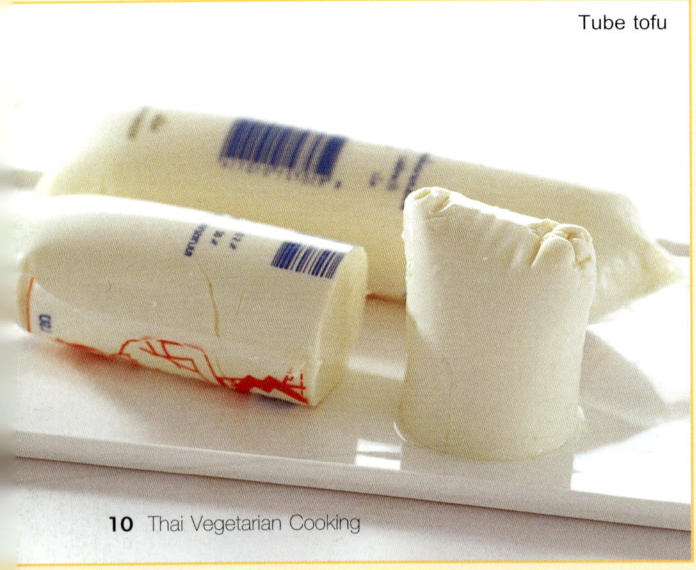
Tube tofu

Tofu string

Dried bean curd skin

Fried dried bean curd skin

Bean Curd Skin This is the cream of constantly-boiled soymilk floated onto the surface, and lifted out in sheets. Bean curd skin can be found in dried and fresh form, but the *dried bean curd skin* is more available. It is popular for soup. *Fresh bean curd skin* can be pressed into various forms and called *hookee*. With chewy texture, *hookee* is a perfect replacement for meat in many Thai dishes. However, it is available only in Chinatown area and some health food shops.

Hookee

Fresh bean curd skin

Textured vegetable protein (TVP)

Tempeh

Textured Vegetable Protein (TVP) A highly processed, chewy product made from soybeans. TVP is generally used for minced meat. In Thai vegetarian cooking it is added to spicy salads, vegetarian fish curry sauce, and stir-fried with holy basil and chili.

Tempeh An Indonesian natural culture of soybeans with chunky, chewy texture. Tempeh is usually cut into slices for stir-fry, deep-fry and grill. It is available only in selected supermarkets and vegetarian food stores.

Thua-nao A traditional food produced from natural culture of soybeans from Northern Thailand. *Thua-nao* can be used as main ingredient and seasoning. It is available in dried and wet versions. Before using, the *dried thua-nao* has to be grilled to release aroma. *Thua-nao* can be found in fresh markets in Northern provinces. But in Bangkok it is available only in selected vegetarian food stores.

Dried thua-nao

Basic Recipes

Stock, seasoned ingredients, and curry paste are preparations commonly used in many recipes. For the sake of convenience, these basic recipes are shown here.

Vegetable Stock and Vegetarian Noodle Stock

Vegetable Stock (Version 1)

- 8 cups water
- 1 (50 grams) salted preserved Chinese radish
- 3 coriander roots, bruised
- 1/2 teaspoon black peppercorns, cracked
- 1 (100 grams) onion, quartered

1. Bring a pot of water to the boil over medium heat. Clean salted preserved Chinese radish and put in, followed by coriander roots and peppercorns. When the stock starts boiling, reduce the heat to low and simmer for 30 minutes. Add onion, continue cooking for an hour, remove from the heat.
2. Strain to reserve only the stock.

Vegetable Stock (Version 2)

- 8 cups water
- 1 (50 grams) salted preserved Chinese radish
- 3 coriander roots, bruised
- 1/2 teaspoon black peppercorns, cracked
- 1 onion, cut half lengthwise
- 2-3 tablespoons golden raisin
- 1 (170 grams) red apple, peeled and cut into pieces
- 1/2 cup white jelly fungus, soaked until tender, blanched and torn into small pieces
- 2 teaspoons seasoning sauce
- 2 teaspoons light soy sauce
- 1/4 teaspoon sea salt

1. Bring a pot of water to the boil, using medium heat. Clean salted preserved Chinese radish and put in. Add coriander roots and peppercorns. When the soup boils, reduce to low heat. Simmer for 30 minutes, add onion and continue cooking for another 1 hour. Remove from the heat and strain into another pot.
2. Place the pot of stock over medium heat and bring to the boil. Add in raisin and apple, cook until tender. Add white jelly fungus and return to the boil. Season with seasoning sauce, light soy sauce and salt, stirring to mix well and turn off the heat. This is the perfect stock for wonton soup.

Vegetable Stock (Version 3)

- 1 piece (500 grams) matured wax gourd, peeled
- 16 cups water
- 2 (450-500 grams each) Chinese radishes, sliced
- 1 ear (350 grams) sweet corn, cut into sections
- 2 (50 grams each) salted preserved Chinese radishes
- 1/2 teaspoon black peppercorns, cracked
- 1/4 cup Chinese wolfberry
- 1 teaspoon oil reserved from fried shiitake mushrooms

1. Half the wax gourd, discard seeds and membrane and wash well. Cut into big pieces, put aside.
2. Place a pot of water over medium heat and bring to the boil. Add wax gourd, Chinese radish, sweet corn, salted preserved Chinese radishes and peppercorns. When it boils, turn the heat to low. Simmer for 30-45 minutes, add Chinese wolfberry and cook for a moment. Stir in oil and remove from the heat. Strain.

Vegetarian Noodle Stock (Version 1)

- 10 cups vegetable stock (version 1 page 13)
- 1 tablespoon sweet dark soy sauce
- 1 piece (2" long) mature galangal, bruised
- 2 stems lemongrass, cut into 3" sections and bruised, 10 kaffir lime leaves, torn
- 1 tablespoon black peppercorns, cracked
- 5 sticks (1" long) roasted cinnamon
- 1 roasted star anise, 2 roasted cardamom pods
- 1 tablespoon roasted coriander seeds
- 1/2 tablespoon roasted cumin

- Place a pot of stock over high heat and bring to the boil. Add sweet dark soy sauce, galangal, lemongrass, kaffir lime leaves, peppercorns, cinnamon, star anise, cardamon pods, coriander seeds and cumin, boil for 15 minutes. Reduce to low heat, simmer for another 30 minutes. Discard the solid ingredients and continue simmering until the stock becomes sweet and fragrant. Turn off the heat.

Note: *All solid ingredients must be removed before simmering or the stock will be bitter.*

Vegetarian Noodle Stock (Version 2)

15 cloves Thai garlic, peeled
3 coriander roots, sliced
1 teaspoon black peppercorns
12 cups vegetable stock (version 1 page 13)
2 (350-400 grams each) Chinese radishes, sliced
1/2 (200 grams) Sriracha pineapple, sliced
2 tomatoes
1 piece (2" long) mature galangal, bruised
5 kaffir lime leaves, torn
5 large pandanus leaves, tied
7 straw mushrooms, halved
50 grams angel mushrooms, torn
1/2 teaspoon sea salt
2 tablespoons light soy sauce
1/4 cup rock sugar
muslin for wrapping

1. Pound garlic, coriander roots and peppercorns well. Spoon the mixture into muslin and tie to form a bouquet garni.
2. Place a pot of stock over high heat and bring to the boil. Add Chinese radish, pineapple, tomatoes, galangal, kaffir lime leaves, pandanus leaves, straw mushrooms, angel mushrooms and bouquet garni, cook until it boils again. Reduce to low heat. Season with salt, light soy sauce and rock sugar. Gently simmer over low heat until the stock is sweet and fragrant. Turn off the heat.

Vegetarian Noodle Stock (Version 3)

25 cloves Thai garlic, peeled
5 coriander roots, sliced
2 teaspoons black peppercorns
4 star anises, 2 sticks (2" long) cinnamon
12 cups water or vegetable stock (version 1 page 13)
2 (350-400 grams each) Chinese radishes, sliced
1/2 (200 grams) Sriracha pineapple, sliced
2 tomatoes
1 piece (2" long) mature galangal, bruised
5 kaffir lime leaves, torn
7 large pandanus leaves, tied
7 straw mushrooms, halved
50 grams angel mushrooms, torn
1 teaspoon sea salt
1 1/2 tablespoons light soy sauce
4 cubes red fermented tofu, mashed
1 tablespoon+1 teaspoon sweet dark soy sauce
1/4 cup rock sugar
muslin for wrapping

1. In a mortar, pound garlic, coriander roots and peppercorns well. Dip out and put onto a piece of muslin, add star anises and cinnamon. Tie to form a bouquet garni.
2. Bring a pot of water or stock to the boil over high heat. Add Chinese radish, pineapple, tomatoes, galangal, kaffir lime leaves, pandanus leaves, straw mushrooms, angel mushrooms and bouquet garni. When it boils, turn the heat to low. Season well with salt, light soy sauce, red fermented tofu, sweet dark soy sauce and rock sugar. Continue simmering until the stock becomes fragrant and sweet. Turn off the heat.

Seasoned Ingredients

Savory Shiitake Mushroom (Version 1)

8 dried shiitake mushrooms
1 cup vegetable oil
1 cup water or vegetable stock (version 3 page 14)
1 tablespoon light soy sauce
2 tablespoons vegetarian oyster sauce
1/4 teaspoon sea salt, 1/2 teaspoon sugar
1 piece (1" long) mature ginger, bruised

1. Clean shiitake mushrooms well, soak in a bowl of water until tender. Remove and squeeze to dry. Fry in hot oil over moderate heat until golden. Remove and put aside.
2. Drain away the oil and reserve only 1 tablespoon in the frying pan. Reduce the heat to low, pour in water or stock. Season to taste with light soy sauce, oyster sauce, salt and sugar. Add fried shiitake mushrooms and toss to coat. Add ginger, stir well. Cover and simmer until the sauce reduces and the mushrooms are cooked and tender, turn off the heat.

Savory Shiitake Mushroom (Version 2)

8 dried shiitake mushrooms, 1 cup vegetable oil
1 cup water or vegetable stock (version 3 page 14)
1 tablespoon light soy sauce
1/2 tablespoon seasoning sauce
1 tablespoon palm sugar, 1/4 teaspoon sea salt
1/4 teaspoon freshly ground black pepper

1. Wash shiitake mushrooms well and soak in a bowl of water until tender. Squeeze to dry, fry in hot oil over moderate heat until just golden. Put aside.
2. Drain away the oil and reserve only 1 tablespoon in the frying pan. Turn the heat to low, pour in water or vegetable stock. Season with light soy sauce, seasoning sauce, palm sugar, salt and black pepper. Stir well. When the sauce boils, add in fried shiitake mushrooms. Toss to coat well, cover. Simmer until the mushrooms are cooked through and absorb most of the sauce. Turn off the heat.

Braised Shiitake Mushroom

10 dried shiitake mushrooms
2 tablespoons vegetable oil
2 tablespoons light soy sauce
1 teaspoon sugar
1 cup liquid reserved from soaking shiitake mushrooms

- Clean shiitake mushrooms well, soak in a bowl of water until tender. Squeeze to dry and trim off hard stems, reserve the soaked liquid. Fry mushrooms in oil over medium heat until fragrant. Season well with light soy sauce and sugar. Add reserved liquid, simmer over low heat until the sauce reduces and the mushrooms are cooked and tender. Turn off the heat.

Salty Textured Vegetable Protein

9 cloves Thai garlic, peeled
2 coriander roots, sliced
1/2 teaspoon black peppercorns, cracked
50 grams small-sized textured vegetable protein (TVP)
2 cups vegetable oil
1 cup water or vegetable stock (version 1 page 13)

Savory shiitake mushroom (Version 1)

Savory shiitake mushroom (Version 2)

Braised shiitake mushroom

1 tablespoon light soy sauce
$1\frac{1}{2}$ teaspoons seasoning sauce
1 tablespoon palm sugar
$\frac{1}{4}$ teaspoon sea salt

1. Pound garlic, coriander roots and peppercorns thoroughly with a mortar and a pestle. Put aside.
2. Bring a pot of water to the boil over medium heat. Add TVP and cook until tender. Transfer to soak in cold water for a few minutes, squeeze to dry. Fry in hot oil until lightly golden. Put aside.
3. Drain away the oil and reserve only 2 tablespoons in the frying pan. Sauté the pounded mixture until fragrant. Add fried TVP and stir well. Add water or vegetable stock and turn to low heat. Season with light soy sauce, seasoning sauce, palm sugar and salt. Toss to combine. Cover and continue cooking until the sauce reduces and TVP are done and tender. Turn off the heat.

Sweet Textured Vegetable Protein

9 cloves Thai garlic, peeled
3 coriander roots, sliced
$\frac{1}{2}$ teaspoon black peppercorns, cracked
50 grams small-sized textured vegetable protein (TVP), 2 cups vegetable oil
1 cup water or vegetable stock (version 1 page 13)
1 tablespoon+2 teaspoons light soy sauce
1 tablespoon+2 teaspoons seasoning sauce
1 teaspoon sweet dark soy sauce
2 tablespoons palm sugar, $\frac{1}{4}$ teaspoon sea salt

1. Thoroughly pound garlic, coriander roots and peppercorns to a fine paste.
2. Place a pot of water over medium heat and bring to the boil. Add TVP and cook until tender. Transfer to soak in a bowl of cold water, squeeze to dry. Fry in hot oil until lightly golden. Remove and set aside.
3. Drain away the oil and reserve only 2 tablespoons in the frying pan. Sauté the garlic paste until fragrant. Add fried TVP and stir well. Add water or stock, turn to low heat. Season with light soy sauce, seasoning sauce, sweet dark soy sauce, palm sugar and salt, stir to combine. Cover and continue cooking until TVP absorbs most of the liquid. Turn off the heat.

Mee kueng

4 cups bread flour, 1 cup water
1 teaspoon sea salt

1. Sift the flour twice. Combine water and salt together and put aside.
2. In a mixer fitted with the hook attachment, put in sifted flour. Beat at a medium speed; gradually add water while beating until all the water is used up. Beat until smooth dough forms and pulls away from the bowl sides.
3. Wash the dough under running water until only *mee kueng* remains and the water is clear. Leave *mee kueng* in a bowl of water for 1-2 hours to obtain soft and chewy texture.
4. To shape *mee kueng*:

a) Coat a chopstick with *mee kueng* dough. Tie a string diagonally around the log and cook in hot boiling water until done. Remove the string and the chopstick.
b) Roll *mee kueng* dough into balls of several sizes. Cook in the hot boiling water until done.
(Make 8-10 balls)

Salty textured vegetable protein

Sweet textured vegetable protein

Mee kueng

Vegetarian Curry Paste

Red Curry Paste

- 5 dried red spur chilies, seeded, soaked until tender
- 1 teaspoon sea salt
- 1 teaspoon mature galangal, finely sliced
- 1 tablespoon lemongrass, finely sliced
- 1 teaspoon kaffir lime rind, finely sliced
- 2 teaspoons coriander root, sliced
- 5 peppercorns, 10 cloves Thai garlic, peeled
- 5 shallots, sliced
- 1 tablespoon ground roasted coriander seeds
- 1 teaspoon roasted cumin
- 1 teaspoon vegetarian shrimp paste or dark fermented soybean

- In a mortar, pound dried chilies and salt to a fine paste. Add galangal, lemongrass, kaffir lime rind, coriander root, peppercorns and garlic. Pound well, then add shallots, coriander seeds, cumin, vegetarian shrimp paste or dark fermented soybean. Continue pounding until a fine paste is obtained.

Southern Red Curry Paste

- 40 grams dried hot chilies
- 1/2 teaspoon sea salt
- 10 fresh red hot chilies
- 1 tablespoon mature galangal, finely sliced
- 2 stems lemongrass, finely sliced
- 1 teaspoon kaffir lime rind, finely sliced
- 1/2 tablespoon black peppercorns
- 30 grams Thai garlic, peeled
- 2 shallots, sliced
- 1 piece (1" long) fresh turmeric
- 1 tablespoon vegetarian shrimp paste or dark fermented soybean

- Pound dried chilies and salt with a mortar and a pestle thoroughly. Add fresh chilies, galangal, lemongrass, kaffir lime rind, peppercorns and garlic. Pound finely, add shallots, turmeric, and vegetarian shrimp paste or fermented soybean. Continue pounding to obtain a fine paste.

Sour Curry Paste

- 5 dried red spur chilies, seeded, soaked until tender
- 1/2 teaspoon sea salt
- 19 cloves Thai garlic, peeled
- 1/2 teaspoon kaffir lime rind, finely sliced
- 1 wild ginger root, sliced
- 3 shallots, sliced
- 1 tablespoon vegetarian shrimp paste or dark fermented soybean

- Pound dried chilies and salt together well. Add garlic and kaffir lime rind, pound to a fine paste. Add wild ginger, shallots and vegetarian shrimp paste or dark fermented soybean. Pound until a fine paste is obtained.

Green Curry Paste

- 15 small green hot chilies
- 29 large green hot chilies
- 1/2 teaspoon sea salt
- 5 peppercorns
- 1 tablespoon mature galangal, finely sliced
- 2 tablespoons lemongrass, finely sliced
- 1 teaspoon kaffir lime rind, finely sliced
- 1 teaspoon coriander root, sliced
- 20 grams Thai garlic, peeled
- 7 shallots, sliced
- 1 tablespoon vegetarian shrimp paste or dark fermented soybean

- In a mortar, put in both kinds of chilies, salt and peppercorns, pound thoroughly. Add galangal, lemongrass, kaffir lime rind, coriander root and garlic. Pound well. Add shallots and vegetarian shrimp paste or dark fermented soybean. Continue pounding to a fine paste.

Mussamun Curry Paste

- 3 dried red spur chilies, seeded, soaked until tender
- 1 teaspoon sea salt
- 1 teaspoon sliced mature galangal, roasted
- 1 tablespoon sliced lemongrass, roasted
- 2 cloves roasted Thai garlic
- 5 roasted shallots
- 1 teaspoon pepper
- 1 tablespoon roasted coriander seeds, ground
- 1 teaspoon roasted cumin, ground
- 2 roasted cloves, ground
- 1 teaspoon vegetarian shrimp paste or dark fermented soybean

- Pound dried chilies and salt thoroughly in a mortar. Add galangal, lemongrass, garlic and shallots, pound to fine paste. Add pepper, coriander seeds, cumin, cloves and vegetarian shrimp paste or dark fermented soybean. Continue pounding to a fine paste.

Southern Yellow Curry Paste

- 40 large red hot chilies
- 1/2 teaspoon sea salt
- 1 stem lemongrass, finely sliced
- 25 cloves Thai garlic, peeled
- 1 piece (2" long) fresh turmeric
- 2 teaspoons vegetarian shrimp paste or dark fermented soybean

- Pound chilies and salt finely. Add lemongrass, garlic and turmeric, pound well. Add vegetarian shrimp paste or dark fermented soybean and pound until a fine paste is obtained.

Vegetarian Fish's Entrails Curry Paste

40-50 dried hot chilies
2 teaspoons sea salt
1/2 teaspoon mature galangal, finely sliced
3 stems lemongrass, finely sliced
1 tablespoon kaffir lime rind, finely sliced
15 peppercorns
15 cloves Thai garlic, peeled
1 piece (1" long) fresh turmeric
4 shallots, sliced

- In a mortar, put in dried chilies and salt, pound thoroughly. Add galangal, lemongrass, kaffir lime rind, peppercorns and garlic, followed by turmeric and shallots, pound to a fine paste after each adding.

Jungle Curry Paste

10 dried red spur chilies, seeded, soaked until tender
1/2 teaspoon sea salt
30 dried hot chilies
2 tablespoons mature galangal, finely sliced
4 stems lemongrass, finely sliced
2 teaspoons kaffir lime rind, finely sliced
1 tablespoon coriander root, sliced
1 teaspoon peppercorns
1/4 cup Thai garlic, peeled
3 shallots, sliced
1 tablespoon vegetarian shrimp paste or dark fermented soybean

- Pound dried chilies and salt finely. Add dried hot chilies, galangal, lemongrass, kaffir lime rind, coriander root, peppercorns and garlic, pound to a fine paste. Add shallots and vegetarian shrimp paste or dark fermented soybean. Continue pounding until well-mixed and a smooth paste is obtained.

Recipes

Spring Rolls with Vegetable Filling

(paw-pia thod sai phak)

- 100 grams dried mung bean noodles
- 100 grams hard white tofu, diced
- $\frac{1}{2}$ cup dried shiitake mushrooms, soaked until tender and cut into strips
- 1 cup bean sprouts, rooted
- 100 grams cabbage, shredded
- 100 grams carrot, shredded
- $\frac{1}{2}$ cup dried black ear mushrooms, soaked until tender and shredded
- 1 teaspoon black pepper
- $\frac{1}{4}$ cup+2$\frac{1}{2}$ tablespoons light soy sauce
- 3 tablespoons sugar
- 1 tablespoon garlic, chopped
- 4 cups vegetable oil
- 200 grams spring roll sheets (5" in diameter)
- spring onion, sweet basil sprig and red cabbage for garnish

Dipping sauce

- $\frac{1}{4}$ cup vinegar
- $\frac{1}{4}$ cup water
- $\frac{1}{2}$ cup sugar
- 1 teaspoon sea salt
- 1 red spur chili, seeded and pounded finely
- A mixture of 1 tablespoon of tapioca flour and 2 tablespoons of water

1. To prepare the dipping sauce: Combine vinegar, water, sugar, salt and pounded spur chili in a sauce pot. Place the pot over medium heat and cook until boiling. Stir in tapioca batter and cook until the sauce is thickened.
2. Soak mung bean noodles in water for 12 minutes until tender. Drain and cut into short sections. In a mixing bowl, combine mung bean noodles, tofu, shiitake mushrooms, bean sprouts, cabbage, carrot, ear mushrooms, pepper, light soy sauce and sugar together.
3. Fry chopped garlic with $\frac{1}{4}$ cup of oil over medium heat until golden and fragrant. Add the mixture prepared in step 2 and cook until everything is done. This is the filling.
4. Place spring roll sheet on a flat surface, spoon about 2 tablespoons of the filling onto the centre of the sheet. Fold the left and right sides over the filling and roll to cover. Brush egg white along the edge and seal tightly. Continue until the filling is used up.
5. Place a pan with the remaining oil over medium-low heat. When the oil is hot deep-fry spring rolls until golden on all sides. Remove and drain.
6. Arrange spring rolls on a serving dish and garnish with spring onion, sweet basil sprig and red cabbage. Enjoy with the dipping sauce. (Make 17 rolls)

Buy the freshly-made spring roll sheets with a smooth surface. Always keep them in a sealed plastic bag. The sheets will crack easily thus being unable to wrap over the filling if they are exposed to the air. Brush the edge of the sheet with egg white to seal tightly.

Crispy Rice Crackers with Minced Tofu Dip

(khao-tang naa-tang)

- 2 cups vegetable oil
- 100 grams rice crackers
- 1 tablespoon garlic, sliced
- 1 teaspoon coriander root, finely sliced
- 1/4 teaspoon pepper
- 1 dried red spur chili
- 1 cup coconut cream
- 3/4 cup semi-hard white tofu, minced
- 1/4 cup carrot, chopped
- 100 grams straw mushrooms, chopped
- 3 tablespoons sugar
- 3 tablespoons light soy sauce
- 1/4 teaspoon sea salt
- 1/4 cup ground roasted peanut
- 2 tablespoons shallot, sliced
- coriander and red chili strips for garnish

1. Preheat the oil in a pan over medium heat. Add small amount of rice crackers at a time, deep-fry until golden on both sides. Remove and drain.
2. In a mortar, pound garlic, coriander root, pepper and dried spur chili to a fine mixture. Boil coconut cream in another pan over medium heat until boiling and oil surfaces. Put in the garlic mixture and cook until fragrant. Add tofu, carrot and straw mushrooms. When everything is done, season to taste with sugar, light soy sauce and salt. Stir to combine well. When it boils again, taste and adjust to your liking. The dip should have a perfect balance of sweet and salty. Add ground peanut and shallot, stir to mix well. Turn off the heat.
3. Dip out into a serving dish and garnish with coriander and spur chili strips. Serve with crisp-fried rice crackers.

(Serves 4)

Rice cracker is made by shaping cooked rice to form a round or a square piece, then sun-dry or bake in an oven until it is completely dry. Deep-fry rice crackers in hot oil until golden and crispy, lightly press them with a spatula while frying in order to make them fluffy.

Crunchy Lemongrass with Roasted Chili Sauce

(miang ta-khrai)

- 1/2 cup lemongrass, thinly sliced
- 1/4 cup roasted peanut, coarsely ground
- 1/4 cup roasted white sesame seeds
- 1/2 cup crisp-fried sliced shallot
- 1/2 cup mint leaves, shredded
- 1/4 cup spring onion, sliced
- wild pepper leaves for wrapping

Roasted chili sauce

- 3 tablespoons vegetarian roasted chili paste
- 3 tablespoons+1 teaspoon lime juice
- 1 1/2 tablespoons light soy sauce
- 1 1/2 tablespoons palm sugar

1. To prepare roasted chili sauce: Combine roasted chili paste, lime juice, light soy sauce and palm sugar together. Taste and adjust to obtain a perfect balance of sour, sweet and salty. Put aside.
2. In a mixing bowl, toss lemongrass, roasted peanut and sesame seeds with the sauce prepared in step 1. Add crisp-fried shallot, mint leaves and spring onion. Toss to mix well. Taste and adjust to your liking. Place about 1 tablespoon of the mixture onto each wild pepper leaf and wrap. Serve immediately.

(Serves 4)

Place a knife at an angle when slicing lemongrass will help you slice more easily. Then squeeze over the lemon juice so that the sliced lemongrass turns light pink. Vegetarian roasted chili paste is available in all vegetarian food stores. Buy the freshly-made one without the oily smell and look for manufacturing date and expiry date on its label.

Fried Bread with Mushroom Spread

(kha-nom-pang naa hed)

- 10 slices (0.5 cm thick) French bread
- 2 coriander roots
- 5 cloves small Thai garlic
- 1 teaspoon pepper
- 3 cups vegetable oil
- 1/4 cup onion, coarsely chopped
- 150 grams straw mushrooms, thinly sliced
- 1 egg yolk
- 1 tablespoon light soy sauce
- 1/4 teaspoon sugar
- 1 tablespoon tempura flour
- 1/4 cup spring onion, white part only, sliced
- 2 tablespoons spring onion, sliced
- 1 teaspoon black peppercorn, cracked
- 1 egg, lightly beaten
- coriander leaves and lemon slices for garnish

Either French bread or sandwich bread can be used for this recipe. Bake or air-dry the bread until it is almost dry so that it will not absorb the oil when being fried. Deep-fry the toast in small quantities at a time in order to maintain the oil temperature.

1. Preheat the oven at 160 °C for 10-15 minutes. Bake the French bread until it is slightly dry, bring out of the oven and put aside. Alternatively, the bread can be air-dried (Dry bread will not absorb the oil when being fried).
2. In a mortar, pound coriander roots, garlic and pepper to a fine paste. Preheat a pan with 1 tablespoon of oil over medium heat. Sauté the coriander paste until fragrant. Add onion and continue cooking until done and clear. Add straw mushrooms, stir-fry until cooked through then turn off the heat. Transfer to a mixing bowl and allow to cool down slightly. Add in egg yolk, light soy sauce, sugar, tempura flour and the white part of spring onion. Toss to combine.
3. Spread about 1 tablespoon of the mixture on each slice of toast, sprinkle sliced spring onion and black pepper over before coating the surface with beaten egg. Deep-fry the toast top-side down in hot oil until golden and done. Turn the toast over and fry until golden on both sides. Deep-fry 3 pieces of mushroom toast at a time to maintain the temperature of the oil. Remove and drain. Continue until finished.
4. Arrange attractively on a serving dish and garnish with coriander leaves and lemon slices. Serve at once.

(Make 10 pieces)

Golden Fried Wonton

(kiaw thod)

- 1/2 pack (75 grams) wonton sheet, size 3"x3"
- 3 cups vegetable oil
- shredded red cabbage, shredded carrot and sweet basil sprig for garnish

The filling

- 1/2 teaspoon peppercorns
- 10 cloves Thai garlic, peeled
- 3 coriander roots, sliced
- 2 tablespoons vegetable oil
- 50 grams coarsely chopped abalone mushrooms
- 50 grams coarsely chopped straw mushrooms
- 1/3 cup steamed taro, mashed
- 1/3 cup steamed potato, mashed
- 1/3 cup boiled water chestnut, coarsely chopped
- 1 1/2 teaspoons seasoning sauce
- 1 1/2 teaspoons light soy sauce
- 2-3 tablespoons finely chopped carrot
- 1/4 cup dried shiitake mushrooms, soaked and squeezed to dry then fried until just golden and finely chopped

Hot dipping sauce

- 7 hot chilies
- 20 cloves Thai garlic, peeled
- 1/2 teaspoon sea salt
- 1 tablespoon boiled water
- 2 1/2 tablespoons lime juice
- 1 tablespoon palm sugar

Sweet dipping sauce

- 1 pickled plum, seeded
- 2-3 large red hot chilies
- 1/4 cup sugar
- 3 tablespoons fermented vinegar
- 1/2 teaspoon sea salt

1. To prepare hot dipping sauce: Pound chilies, garlic and salt finely. Transfer to a sauce bowl and stir in water. Season with lime juice and palm sugar, stir to mix well.
2. To prepare sweet dipping sauce: Pound pickled plum and chilies to a fine paste. Transfer to a sauce bowl and put aside. Combine sugar, vinegar and salt in a sauce pot. Cook over low heat until slightly thickened, remove from the heat and mix with pounded plum. Stir well.
3. To prepare the filling: In a mortar, thoroughly pound peppercorns. Add coriander roots and garlic, pound to a fine paste. Sauté the mixture with oil over medium heat until fragrant. Add both mushrooms and cook until done. Add taro, potato and water chestnut. Toss and cook until done. Season with seasoning sauce and light soy sauce, add carrot and fried shiitake mushrooms. Stir-fry until everything is well-combined, remove from the heat and allow to cool.
4. Spread wonton sheet on a flat surface, place 1 teaspoon of the filling onto the centre. Fold the sheet to cover and to form a triangle. Attach both pointed ends together, brush both ends with water and press tightly. Keep in a container and cover with damp cloth to prevent from dryness.
5. Place a frying pan with oil over medium heat until the oil is hot. Fry wontons until cooked through and golden crispy. Remove and drain.
6. Arrange attractively on a serving platter, garnish with red cabbage, carrot and sweet basil sprig. Serve immediately with dipping sauces.

(Makes 15 pieces)

Vegetarian Rolls

(miang sod mang-sa-wi-rad)

- 1 white jelly fungus, soaked until tender
- 1 tablespoon sliced coriander root
- 1 teaspoon peppercorns
- 2 tablespoons Thai garlic, peeled
- 2 tablespoons vegetable oil
- 200 grams chopped straw mushrooms
- 1 piece (130 grams) hard white tofu, cut into small cubes and fried until lightly golden
- 1 tablespoon light soy sauce
- 1 teaspoon sea salt
- 1/2 cup ground roasted rice
- 12 sheets Vietnamese rice wrapper
- Fresh vegetables: wild pepper leaves, lettuce, mint leaves, shredded banana blossom, sliced spring onion, coriander leaves, blanched bean sprouts, etc.
- sweet basil sprig for garnish

Dipping Sauce

- 1/3 cup tamarind juice
- 1/2 cup palm sugar
- 3 tablespoons unbleached sugar
- 2 teaspoons sea salt
- 1/4 cup water
- 9 large red hot chilies, finely pounded
- 1 tablespoon lime juice

1. Trim off the hard base of white jelly fungus. Dip into hot boiling water and cook over medium heat for a moment. Remove and soak in cold water. Squeeze to dry and tear into small pieces.
2. Finely pound coriander root, add peppercorns and garlic and pound to a fine paste.
3. Place a pan with oil over medium heat, sauté the pounded mixture until fragrant. Add straw mushrooms and cook until done. Add fried tofu and white jelly fungus, toss to combine. Season with light soy sauce and salt, toss to combine and turn off the heat. Transfer to a mixing bowl and leave to cool. Add ground roasted rice, toss to mix well (Do not add roasted rice while the filling is still hot as it will not be crispy).
4. To prepare dipping sauce: Combine tamarind juice, palm sugar, sugar, salt and water in a sauce pot. Cook over medium heat until boiling and sugar dissolves. Remove from the heat, stir in pounded chilies. When the sauce is completely cool, add lime juice and stir to mix well.
5. Spread a piece of rice wrapper on a flat surface, sprinkle small amount of water, line all fresh vegetables on the wrapper and top with the filling. Fold the sides and roll tightly.
6. Arrange on a serving dish and garnish with sweet basil sprig. Enjoy with the dipping sauce. (serve the whole rolls or slice into pieces as preferred).

(Serves 6)

Vietnamese rice wrappers are sold in dried form. They are available both round and rectangular shapes. Sprinkle some water to soften them before using, or cover each sheet with wet banana leaf for a few minutes to get the same result.

Steamed Crescents with Mushroom Filling

(khao-kriab-pak-mor sai hed)

The batter

- 1¼ cups rice flour
- ¼ cup tapioca flour
- 1 tablespoon arrow root flour
- 1¼ cups water
- ⅛ teaspoon sea salt
- Fresh vegetables: green ork lettuce and coriander

Mushroom filling

- 1 tablespoon chopped Thai garlic
- 2 tablespoons vegetable oil
- ½ cup fresh shiitake mushrooms, coarsely chopped
- 1 cup straw mushrooms, coarsely chopped
- ½ cup carrot, julienned
- ½ cup pumpkin, julienned
- 2 tablespoons light soy sauce
- 2 teaspoons unbleached sugar
- ⅛ teaspoon sea salt
- ½ teaspoon black pepper
- ¼ cup sliced spring onion, green part only

Dipping sauce

- 1 red spur chili, sliced
- 7 cloves Thai garlic, peeled
- 1 tablespoon+2 teaspoons vinegar
- 1 teaspoon unbleached sugar
- ½ teaspoon sea salt

1. To prepare the batter: Combine all flour in a mixing bowl. Gradually add water and mix until no lump remains. Add all water and salt, stir to mix well and put aside.
2. To prepare mushroom filling: Fry garlic in oil over medium heat until slightly golden. Add shiitake and straw mushrooms, cook until tender. Add carrot and pumpkin and cook until done. Season with light soy sauce, sugar, salt and pepper. Stir to mix well. Taste to your liking and add in spring onion. Remove from the heat and put aside.
3. To prepare dipping sauce: Pound red chili and garlic until fine. Dip out into a sauce dish and stir in vinegar, sugar and salt. The taste should be sour and sweet with a slightly salty and hot taste.
4. Fill half of the pot with water, cover its top with a piece of cheesecloth and tie tightly with the string. Place the pot over medium heat and bring to the boil. Stir the batter before ladle a spoonful onto the cloth. With the back of a ladle, spread to obtain a round and thin sheet. Cover and leave until done. Place 1 tablespoon of the filling at the centre. Wrap to cover the filling with a spatula and remove from the heat. Repeat the same process until the filling is used up (makes about 14 pieces).
5. Arrange stuffed crescents on a serving dish, garnish with hot chilies and serve with fresh vegetables and dipping sauce.

(Serves 2)

Soak a piece of cheesecloth overnight, fold it in half and place over the top of a pot. Tie the cloth tightly and make a hole about 2-3" wide with a sharp knife to help release the steam.

Fried Mushrooms and Tofu with Savory Sauce

(miang hed)

- 4 (10 grams each) dried shiitake mushrooms
- 1 1/2 cups oyster mushrooms, discard stems and torn into strips
- 1 piece (110 grams) semi-hard tofu
- 1/2 teaspoon black peppercorns
- 9 cloves Thai garlic, peeled
- 3 coriander roots, sliced
- 8 straw mushrooms, cut into small pieces
- 1 1/2 tablespoons light soy sauce
- 1/2 teaspoon unbleached sugar
- 1/4 teaspoon sea salt
- 3 cups vegetable oil
- 1/4 cup crisp-fried sliced shallot
- Fresh vegetable: iceberg lettuce

Savory sauce

- 2 1/2 tablespoons palm sugar syrup
- 2 tablespoons+2 teaspoons light soy sauce
- 1 tablespoon roasted shallot, pound finely
- 1 tablespoon roasted garlic, pound finely
- 1/4 cup lime juice

1. To prepare savory sauce: Combine all ingredients together, stir well and put aside.
2. Wash dried shiitake mushrooms and soak until tender. Remove and wash in a solution of tapioca flour and water until is completely clean. Wash again and squeeze to dry. Cut into small pieces and put aside.
3. Steam oyster mushrooms over medium heat until done and tender. Remove and leave to cool.
4. Bring a pot of water to the boil over high heat (add a dash of salt into water). Add in tofu and boil until done and floated to the surface. Remove and cut into small cubes.
5. Finely pound peppercorns, garlic and coriander roots and put aside.
6. In a mixing bowl, combine all mushrooms and tofu together. Add pounded pepper mixture, light soy sauce, sugar and salt. Toss and leave to marinate at a room temperature for 15 minutes.
7. Place a pan with oil over medium heat until the oil is hot. Fry marinated mushrooms until crispy on the outside but is still tender on the inside. Remove and drain.
8. To serve: Ladle fried mushrooms onto iceberg lettuce and place on a serving dish. Sprinkle crisp-fried shallot over the top and serve with the savory sauce.

(Serves 4)

As oyster mushrooms are very juicy, it is recommended to steam them to reduce their moisture and to obtain the crispy texture after being fried. Soak dried shiitake mushrooms until tender before washing in a solution of tapioca flour and water to remove the dirt.

Multi-Grains Pancake

(pancake than-ya-pheud)

- 100 grams mung beans
- 100 grams hulled mung beans
- 1/4 cup uncooked brown rice
- 1/2 ear boiled sweet corn kernels
- 80 grams pumpkin, peeled and cut into small pieces
- 1/2 cup water
- 1 teaspoon sea salt
- 1/2 cup vegetable oil
- 1/2 cup shredded cabbage
- 1/4 cup sliced yard-long bean
- 1 red spur chili, diagonally sliced
- iceberg lettuce for garnish
- chili sauce and tomato ketchup

Dipping Sauce

- 1/4 cup light soy sauce
- 1 1/2 tablespoons lime juice
- 1 1/2 tablespoons brown sugar
- 9 red and green hot chilies, sliced
- 1 spring onion, sliced
- 1 coriander, sliced

1. To prepare dipping sauce: combine light soy sauce, lime juice and sugar in a sauce bowl, stir until dissolved. Add chilies, spring onion and coriander. Stir to combine, put aside.
2. Wash mung beans, hulled mung beans and brown rice. Soak them together in a bowl of water overnight. Wash again and drain.
3. Mash or blend the soaked beans and rice with corn kernels, pumpkin and water to a fine puree. (You can pound them finely before mixing with water, do not add too much liquid as the mixture will be too thin). Transfer the mixture to a bowl and add in salt, stir to combine.
4. Place a non-stick pan over low heat until it is slightly hot. Add 1 tablespoon of oil, pour 1/2 cup of the mixture into the pan and swirl to form a 3" pancake. Arrange shredded cabbage, yard-long bean and chili over the top. Cook until golden then turn it over to fry the other side. Press the pancake lightly with a spatula, add small amount of oil while cooking so that it will not be too hard. Fry until cooked through, remove from the heat. Continue until the mixture is used up.
5. Arrange on a serving dish and garnish with iceberg lettuce. Enjoy while still hot with choices of dipping sauce, chili sauce or tomato ketchup.

(Makes 10 pieces)

This Korean-style multi-grains pancake, or is called *"Pindeto"* in Korean, contains high nutritional value from beans, grains and vegetables.

Spicy Banana Blossom Fritters

(thod-mun hua-plee)

1 large banana blossom
5 cups clear lime liquid (mixing 2 tablespoons of slake lime with 5 cups of water, stir and leave to settle, strain and reserve only the clear liquid)
4 cups vegetable oil

The batter

2 tablespoons all purpose flour
1/2 cup rice flour
1 cup coconut cream
1/2 teaspoon slake lime
1 duck's egg yolk
1/2 teaspoon sea salt
2 tablespoons red curry paste (page 18)
1 tablespoon shredded kaffir lime leaves

Cucumber relish

1/2 cup vinegar
1/2 cup sugar
1/2 teaspoon sea salt
1/2 cup cucumber, thinly sliced
2 red spur chilies, cut into rings
2 tablespoons ground roasted peanuts
1 coriander, leaves only

1. To prepare cucumber relish: Combine vinegar, sugar and salt together and cook over low heat until slightly thickened. Remove from the heat and allow to cool. Pour into a sauce bowl, add cucumber, spur chilies, ground peanuts and coriander leaves just before serving.
2. Discard outer tough leaves of banana blossom until the white heart remains. Cut into thin wedges and immediately soak in a bowl of clear lime liquid (prepared as above). Soak for 30 minutes, remove and drain.
3. To prepare the batter: In a mixing bowl, combine all purpose flour and rice flour together. Gradually add coconut cream, stir until no lumps remain. Add slake lime, egg yolk, salt, red curry paste and kaffir lime leaves and stir to obtain the thick batter.
4. Place a frying pan with oil over medium heat and leave until the oil is hot. Dip banana blossom in the batter and deep-fry in hot oil until golden crispy. Remove and drain. Continue until finished.
5. Arrange on a serving platter and serve immediately with cucumber relish.

(Serves 4)

Slake lime is a mixture of limestone, turmeric and salt. White lime can give the same result as slake lime but a bit stronger. Vegetables soaked in lime liquid will have a crisp texture after cooked.

Three-Flavored Crispy Rice Vermicelli

(mee krob)

- 1/2 pack (85 grams) rice vermicelli
- 4 cups vegetable oil
- 1 egg, lightly beaten
- 2 tablespoons chopped garlic
- 2 tablespoons chopped shallot
- 1/2 piece (125 grams) hard white tofu, cut into small pieces
- 1/4 cup salty textured vegetable protein (TVP) (page 16)
- 2 tablespoons dark fermented soybean
- 2 1/2 tablespoons vinegar
- 1 tablespoon light soy sauce
- 3 tablespoons palm sugar
- 1 teaspoon chili powder
- 1 tablespoon lime juice
- 1 tablespoon *som saa* juice (a kind of citrus with dark green rugged skin)
- 1/2 piece (125 grams) hard white tofu, cut into matchstick-size and fried until lightly golden
- 1 bulb pickled garlic, thinly sliced
- 2 tablespoons *som saa* rind, finely sliced
- 1 red spur chili, shredded
- coriander leaves for garnish
- Condiments: lime wedges, bean sprouts and Chinese chives

1. Soak rice vermicelli in water for 15 minutes, remove and drain.
2. Place a pan with oil over moderate heat. When the oil is hot, fry rice vermicelli, a little at a time, until crispy. Remove and drain. Transfer to a mixing bowl, break to separate and put aside. Pour beaten egg through a colander into the same pan, fry until golden crispy. Remove and drain off excess oil.
3. Drain off the oil and leave only 1/4 cup in the pan. Heat until slightly hot, sauté chopped garlic and shallot until fragrant. Add tofu and salty TVP. Toss to combine. Season with fermented soybean, vinegar, light soy sauce, palm sugar, chili powder and continue cooking until the sauce thickens. Add lime juice and *som saa* juice, cook until it returns to the same thickness. Taste for a balance of sweet, sour and salty. Reduce the heat, add in fried rice vermicelli. Toss quickly to coat, add fried tofu and toss lightly. Turn off the heat.
4. Transfer to a serving dish, top with crisp-fried egg, pickled garlic, *som saa* rind and spur chili slices. Garnish with coriander leaves, place lime wedges, bean sprouts and Chinese chives on the side and serve.

(Serves 4)

Som saa belongs to the citrus family. It has an aromatic sour-sweet flavor with green rugged skin similar to kaffir lime. Both its rind and juice are used in this recipe. *Som saa* is rarely found in general market, but you may find it at Jatujak weekend market and Dheves fresh market.

Sweet Corn Patties

(khao-phoad thod)

- 2 ears (330-350 grams each) sweet corn, kernels only
- 1/4 teaspoon sea salt
- 1/4 teaspoon pepper
- 2 tablespoons tempura flour
- 1 tablespoon rice flour
- 3 tablespoons cold water
- 3 cups vegetable oil
- coriander leaves for garnish
- sweet chili sauce

1. In a mixing bowl, combine corn kernels, salt and pepper together, toss well. Add tempura flour, rice flour and water, toss lightly to combine.
2. Pre-heat a wok of oil over medium heat until the oil is hot. Drop a spoonful of the corn mixture into the oil and deep-fry until golden and cooked through. Remove and drain on absorbent paper. Continue frying until the mixture is used up.
3. Arrange on a serving platter, garnish with coriander leaves and serve immediately with sweet chili sauce.

(Make 10 pieces)

Sweet corn contains a lot of vitamin A, phosphorous and high fibre. Buy those with green husks and fresh hair. If their husks are removed, select those with fresh plump kernels and fully ripe. The starchy juice will come out from the kernels when you pick them with your fingernail.

Golden Seaweed Rolls

(sa-rhai muan song-kreung)

- 2 pieces (150 grams each) soft white tofu, boiled
- 1/2 cup boiled taro, diced
- 1/4 cup boiled green pea
- 1/4 cup boiled carrot, diced
- 1/4 teaspoon sea salt
- 1/4 teaspoon pepper
- 1 teaspoon sugar
- 1 1/2 teaspoons light soy sauce
- 1 teaspoon sesame oil
- 3-4 sheets nori seaweed
- 4 cups vegetable oil
- 1/2 cup all purpose flour
- 1 egg, lightly beaten
- 2 cups breadcrumb
- lemon wedges and coriander leaves for garnish

1. In a mixing bowl: mash soft tofu finely, add taro, green pea and carrot. Season well with salt, pepper, sugar, light soy sauce and sesame oil. Toss well to combine.
2. Place the seaweed on a flat surface, put the filling prepared in step 1 along one side. Wrap and roll tightly to obtain a roll about 1" in diameter. Steam over hot boiling water for 5 minutes or until cooked through, using low heat. Remove and leave to cool completely. Cut diagonally into slices about 1 1/2" thick.
3. Pre-heat a deep frying pan with oil over low heat until the oil is hot. Toss seaweed slices in all purpose flour to coat, dip into beaten egg and coat well with breadcrumb. Deep-fry in hot oil until golden, remove and drain.
4. Arrange nicely on a serving platter, garnish with lemon wedges and coriander leaves. Serve hot with plum sauce.

(Serves 6)

Breadcrumb is available in many supermarkets. You can prepare the fresh crumb easily by yourself. Cut a loaf of French bread into 1/2" slices and chop coarsely in a food processor. It will give a nice golden and crispy texture when deep-fried.

Golden Red Onion Nuggets

(hom thod krob)

- 500 grams red onion
- 1 teaspoon dried hot chilies, roasted and ground
- 1/2 teaspoon turmeric powder
- 1 teaspoon sea salt
- 1/2 cup sticky rice flour
- 1/2 cup rice flour
- 1/4 cup water
- 4 cups vegetable oil

1. Peel red onion and wash well. Thinly slice lengthwise and put into a mixing bowl. Toss lightly with ground chilies, turmeric powder and salt. Gradually add sticky rice flour, followed by rice flour. Toss well before adding water, toss again and leave for 10-15 minutes.
2. Place a frying pan with oil over low heat, when the oil is slightly hot, drop about 2 tablespoons of the red onion mixture into hot oil and fry until golden and no bubbles remain. Remove and drain on absorbent paper.
3. Arrange on a serving dish and serve.

(Serves 4)

Red onion is large-sized shallot, sweeter than the small variety, its fragrance is also weaker. Always use low heat and fry in slightly hot oil. The red onion tends to get burnt quite easily due to its high sugar content.

Mushrooms and Young Coconut Tom Yum

(tom yum hed kub ma-phrao on)

- 50 grams enoki mushrooms
- 3-4 straw mushrooms
- 50 grams oyster mushrooms
- 1 cup water
- 2 cups young coconut juice
- 5 slices young galangal
- 2 stems lemongrass, cut into 1 1/2" pieces and bruised
- 2-3 tomatoes, quartered
- 1 cup young coconut flesh, cut into pieces
- 3-4 shallots, bruised
- 4-5 kaffir lime leaves, torn
- 5-6 hot chilies, lightly crushed
- 1 tablespoon seasoning sauce
- 2 tablespoons light soy sauce
- 1/2 teaspoon sea salt
- 1 saw-leaves coriander plant, chopped
- 2-3 tablespoons lime juice
- saw-leaves coriander and red hot chilies for garnish

1. Clean all mushrooms with a piece of cloth. Cut away the base of enoki mushrooms, trim straw mushrooms and cut into quarters. Tear oyster mushrooms into pieces. Put aside.
2. Combine water and coconut juice in a soup pot and bring to the boil over medium heat. Add galangal and lemongrass, return to boiling. Add mushrooms, tomatoes and coconut flesh. Boil until cooked through. Add shallots, kaffir lime leaves and hot chilies. Season with seasoning sauce, light soy sauce and salt. Stir to mix well, turn off the heat. Add in saw-leaves coriander and lime juice.
3. Divide among serving bowls, garnish with saw-leaves coriander and chilies before serving.

(Serves 3-4)

The fragrant sweet flesh and juice from young coconut always give an aromatic sweetness to many dishes. It contains useful medium-chain saturated fat which helps to stimulate metabolism and does not affect the cholesterol level.

Vegetarian Tom Yum Kung

(tom yum kung je nam khon)

- 2 cups water or noodle stock (version 2 page 15)
- 7 slices young galangal
- 2 stems lemongrass, diagonally sliced
- 3 kaffir lime leaves, torn
- 1 bulb pickled garlic, bruised
- 10 straw mushrooms, halved
- 1 tablespoon vegetarian roasted chili paste
- 1/4 cup+1 1/2 tablespoons light soy sauce
- 1/2 teaspoon sea salt
- 1/4 teaspoon sugar
- 3 tablespoons lime juice
- 5 vegetarian prawns
- 1 1/2 cups coconut milk
- 7 hot chilies, pounded
- 2 coriander plants, cut into 1/2" slices
- kaffir lime leaves, coriander leaves, diagonally sliced lemongrass and hot chilies for garnish

1. In a soup pot, pour in water or stock and bring to the boil over medium heat. Add galangal, lemongrass, kaffir lime leaves and pickled garlic. When it boils again, add straw mushrooms and cook until just done. Season with roasted chili paste, light soy sauce, salt, sugar and lime juice. Stir to combine. The taste should be sour and salty. Add vegetarian prawns and cook for further 3 minutes until they are done. Add coconut milk and cook until boiling. Add hot chilies and coriander, turn off the heat.
2. Dip out into a serving bowl, garnish with kaffir lime leaves, coriander leaves, lemongrass and hot chilies. Serve hot.

(Serves 4)

Vegetarian prawns are made from konjac shaping and coloring to resemble real prawns. Konjac is known as health food, it contains glucomannan which is the natural fibre that helps to ease constipation, reduce blood pressure, cholesterol and blood sugar.

Vegetarian Coconut Galangal Soup

(tom khaa tao-hoo kub hed)

- 1 piece (150 grams) semi-hard white tofu
- 1 cup coconut cream
- 2 cups coconut milk
- 7 slices young galangal
- 1 stalk lemongrass, cut into 1" sections and bruised
- 4 kaffir lime leaves, torn
- 3 tablespoons light soy sauce
- 1 teaspoon sea salt
- 2 1/2 teaspoons sugar
- 2 1/2 tablespoons lime juice
- 100 grams straw mushrooms, halved
- 150 grams angel mushrooms, torn
- 9 hot chilies, crushed
- 1 teaspoon oil reserved from vegetarian roasted chili paste
- kaffir lime leaves, diagonally sliced lemongrass and coriander leaves for garnish

1. Bring a pot of water (with small amount of salt) to the boil over high heat. Cook tofu until floated to the surface (its texture will become firm and chewy). Remove and cut into pieces.
2. Combine coconut cream and coconut milk in a soup pot and boil over medium heat. When boiling, add galangal, lemongrass and kaffir lime leaves. When it boils again and smells fragrant, add cooked tofu. Season to taste with light soy sauce, salt, sugar and lime juice. Cook until the tofu is tender, then add straw mushrooms and angel mushrooms. Continue cooking until everything is done, stir in hot chilies and oil reserved from vegetarian roasted chili paste. Turn off the heat.
3. Dip out into a serving bowl and garnish with kaffir lime leaves, lemongrass and coriander leaves. Enjoy while hot.

(Serves 4)

An aromatic cream soup with a perfect combination of salty, sour and slightly hot tastes is made by cooking slices of young galangal with lemongrass and kaffir lime leaves in coconut soup. Cooked galangal is edible; its pungent taste can relieve the rich and creamy aftertaste.

Thai Vegetable Soup

(kaeng liang)

- 7 cups water
- 1 teaspoon sea salt
- 1/2 cup pumpkin, cut into pieces
- 1 (150 grams) bottle gourd, cut into pieces
- 1/2 cup corn kernels
- 1/2 head banana blossom
- 1/2 (175 grams) angle gourd, cut into pieces
- 1 1/2 tablespoons seasoning sauce
- 1 1/2 tablespoons light soy sauce
- 1/2 teaspoon palm sugar
- 2 cups ivy gourd, tips and leaves only
- 1 cup *phak waan*, tips and leaves only
- 1 cup acacia leaves
- 1 cup hairy basil leaves

Peppery mixture

- 1/2 tablespoon black peppercorns
- 1 wild ginger head
- 7 wild ginger roots, sliced
- 7 cloves Thai garlic, peeled
- 6 shallots, sliced
- 10 green and red hot chilies
- 5 straw mushrooms, halved
- 20 grams abalone mushrooms, torn
- 20 grams oyster mushrooms, torn
- 1 tablespoon vegetarian shrimp paste
- 2 tablespoons dark fermented soybean

1. To make peppery mixture: In a mortar, thoroughly pound peppercorns. Add both parts of wild ginger, garlic, shallots and hot chilies, pound to a fine paste. Add mushrooms, pound finely after each adding. Add shrimp paste and fermented soybean, continue pounding until a fine mixture is obtained.
2. Place a pot of water over medium heat and bring to the boil. Add salt and the peppery mixture, stir well. When the soup is boiling, add pumpkin, bottle gourd and corn kernels. Boil until all vegetables are cooked. Diagonally slice banana blossom and quickly add into the pot. Press the banana blossom to immerse in the soup in order to prevent them from discoloration. When it is heated through, add angle gourd. Season with seasoning sauce, light soy sauce and palm sugar. When it boils again, add ivy gourd, *phak waan*, acacia leaves, hairy basil leaves and turn off the heat.
3. Dip out into a serving bowl and enjoy while hot.

(Serves 4-6)

The peppery mixture is the key ingredient that enhances the taste of this soup. It also provides essential amino acid gain from various kinds of mushroom added in its mixture.

Bitter Gourd Soup with Pickled Mustard Green

(ma-ra tom phak-kaad-dong)

- 7 dried shiitake mushrooms, soaked until tender
- 4 cups vegetable oil
- 1 (600 grams) bitter gourd
- 12 cups water
- 25 cloves Thai garlic, peeled
- 5 coriander roots, bruised
- 2 slices (1" long) mature ginger
- 1 teaspoon cracked black peppercorn
- 250 grams pickled mustard green, cut into 2" pieces
- 1 can (230 grams) pickled mustard green
- 7 straw mushrooms, halved
- 50 grams dried bean curd skin, broken into pieces and fried
- 1/4 cup light soy sauce
- 3 tablespoons seasoning sauce
- 1 tablespoon palm sugar
- 2 teaspoons sea salt
- 5 dried red spur chilies, cut into 1" pieces and fried

Bitter gourd, the fruit which its bitterness is caused by an alkaloid called momodicine, can help to stimulate appetite and is also a mild laxative. Select fresh mature fruit with a light green to creamy white color and light rugged skin. Its flesh will not be too bitter.

1. Wash shiitake mushrooms and soak until tender. Remove and squeeze to dry, cut away hard stems. Fry in hot oil over medium heat until golden and fragrant. Put aside. (Fried shiitake mushrooms will provide stronger aroma with a firm and chewy texture).
2. Wash bitter gourd and pat-dry. Fry the whole fruit in hot oil over high heat for a moment. Remove and soak in a bowl of cold water. Cut across into sections about 2" long, then cut into quarters. Discard seeds and membrane, put aside.
3. Bring a pot of water to the boil over medium heat. Add garlic, coriander roots, ginger, black peppercorn, shiitake mushrooms and pickled mustard green. When the soup boils, reduce to low heat and simmer for 15-20 minutes until the vegetables are tender. Add in bitter gourd, canned pickled mustard green, straw mushrooms and bean curd skin. When the soup becomes boiling, season to taste with light soy sauce, seasoning sauce, palm sugar and salt. Continue simmering for 1 hour or until the bitter gourd is cooked through and tender. Add fried chilies, stir to combine, turn off the heat.
4. Dip out into a serving bowl, serve hot.

(Serves 8-10)

Note: Do not cook with high heat as the soup will become cloudy.

Seaweed Soup

(kaeng jeud sa-rhai)

- 5 dried shiitake mushrooms
- 1 cup vegetable oil
- 25 grams dried lily flowers
- 5 cups vegetable stock (version 1 page 13)
- 60 grams golden raisin
- 100 grams straw mushrooms, cut into wedges
- 1/2 tablespoon sea salt
- 1 tablespoon light soy sauce
- 1 1/2 tablespoons seasoning sauce
- 100 grams enoki mushrooms, cut away hard base
- 1 tube (220 grams) soft tofu, cut into thick slices
- 50 grams *phak waan*, leaves and tips only
- 50 grams ivy gourd, leaves and tips only
- 1/2 (85 grams) red apple, peeled and cut into pieces
- 1/2 pack (50 grams) unbleached mung bean noodles, soaked until tender and cut into sections
- 2 sheets (20 grams each) soup seaweed, grilled until fragrant

1. Wash shiitake mushrooms, soak until soft and squeeze to dry. Trim off hard stems, and fry in hot oil over medium heat until fragrant. Put aside.
2. Wash dried lily flowers and soak until tender. Squeeze, and tie to form a knot. Put aside.
3. Place a pot of vegetable stock over medium heat, add raisin, fried shiitake mushrooms and straw mushrooms. Cook until the mushrooms are done. Season with salt, light soy sauce and seasoning sauce. Stir to mix well. Add enoki mushrooms, tofu and lily flowers. When the vegetables are done and tender, add *phak waan*, ivy gourd, apple and mung bean noodles. Continue cooking until everything is done, turn off the heat. Tear grilled seaweed into pieces and add into the soup.
4. Separate among soup bowls and serve hot.

(Serves 6)

Seaweed contains high fibre which can ease constipation, helps to cure gastric ulcer and prevent cancer. However, it is not recommended for those who suffer from gout disease or rheumatism.

Wax Gourd Soup with Pickled Lime

(fuk toon ma-nao dong)

- 1 kilogram wax gourd
- 4 1/2 cups water or vegetable stock (version 1 page 13)
- 2 cups water reserved from soaked shiitake mushrooms
- 4 dried shiitake mushrooms (about 2" in diameter), soaked until tender and fried
- 1 tablespoon Thai garlic, lightly crushed
- 3 coriander roots
- 1/4 teaspoon black peppercorn, cracked
- 2 tablespoons light soy sauce
- 1 tablespoon seasoning sauce
- 2 teaspoons brown sugar
- 3 tablespoons liquid reserved from pickled lime
- 1 pickled lime
- 1 spring onion, sliced
- 1 coriander, sliced
- pepper

1. Clean wax gourd, peel and cut into halves. Discard seeds and membrane, cut into large pieces and put aside.
2. In a soup pot, combine water or stock with water reserved from soaked shiitake mushrooms. Place the pot over medium heat and add in wax gourd, fried shiitake mushrooms, garlic, coriander roots and peppercorn. Cook until boiling. Season with light soy sauce, seasoning sauce and sugar. Continue cooking until the wax gourd is cooked through and the soup is clear. Add pickled lime and its liquid. The taste should be sour and salty.
3. Ladle into a serving bowl. Sprinkle pepper over and garnish with sliced spring onion and coriander. Serve hot.

(Serves 4)

Lime that is preserved in fish sauce will be sour, salty and slightly sweet, while those preserved in brine will be just sour and salty. Always cook the soup over low heat as the pickled lime will not be broken or give a bitter taste.

Braised Tofu in Five Chinese Spices

(pha-lo tao-hoo)

- 1 piece (200 grams) hard white tofu
- 1/4 cup palm sugar
- 2 cups water
- 1 stick (1") cinnamon, roasted
- 1 star anise, roasted
- 1/2 teaspoon five Chinese spices powder
- 3 coriander roots, bruised
- 7 cloves small Thai garlic, crushed
- 1/2 teaspoon peppercorn, cracked
- 1 tablespoon light soy sauce
- 1 tablespoon seasoning sauce
- 1/2 teaspoon sea salt
- Chinese celery sprig for garnish

The marinade for tofu

- 1 teaspoon light soy sauce
- 1 teaspoon seasoning sauce
- 1/4 teaspoon sugar
- 1/4 teaspoon ground black pepper

1. Bring a pot of water (with small amount of salt) over high heat. Add in tofu and boil until done and floated to the surface (in order to obtain a firm and chewy texture). Remove and put aside.
2. Cut boiled tofu into pieces and put into a mixing bowl. Marinate with light soy sauce, seasoning sauce, sugar and black pepper. Toss to coat, pan-fry in hot oil until golden on all sides.
3. In a pot, add in palm sugar and place over low heat. When it melts and starts caramelized, pour in water. Add cinnamon, star anise, five Chinese spices, coriander roots, garlic and peppercorn. When it boils, season with light soy sauce, seasoning sauce and salt. Add fried tofu and simmer until the tofu absorbs the sauce and is tender. Turn off the heat.
4. Ladle into a serving dish and garnish with Chinese celery sprig. Serve hot.

(Serves 4)

Marinate the tofu and pan-fry until it is golden and fragrant will make the tofu tasty and not being soggy when cooked. Always roast the spices before adding to the soup in order to fully obtain their fragrance.

Braised Hookee in Soy Sauce

(hookee tom see-ew)

- 2 pieces (250 grams each) *hookee*
- 3 cups vegetable oil
- 4 cups water
- 3/4 cup coca cola
- 5 dried shiitake mushrooms, soaked until tender
- 1/4 cup light soy sauce
- 2 teaspoons sweet dark soy sauce
- 1 teaspoon sea salt
- 40 grams rock sugar
- Chinese celery sprigs for garnish

1. Wash *hookee*, cut into pieces and drain. Place a wok of oil over high heat and wait until the oil is very hot, fry *hookee* until lightly golden on all sides. Remove and drain.
2. Bring a pot of water to the boil over medium heat. Add fried *hookee* and coca cola, cook until boiling. Reduce the heat to medium-low, add shiitake mushrooms and cook for a few minutes. Season with light soy sauce, sweet dark soy sauce, salt and sugar. Simmer for 1 hour or until everything is cooked and tender. Remove from the heat.
3. Ladle into a serving dish and garnish with Chinese celery sprigs. Best when serve hot.

(Serves 6)

Hookee is made by wrapping the fresh bean curd skin with a piece of muslin and tied tightly to form various shapes such as a stick resembles sausage, or a lobed ball resembles a pumpkin. It is preferably fried before adding to soup, spicy salad or curry in order to obtain an aromatic and firm texture.

Grilled Long Green Eggplant Salad

(yum ma-kheu-yao)

2 (200 grams each) long green eggplants
1 piece (150 grams) soft white tofu
2 cups vegetable oil
5 shallots, sliced thinly
2 spring onions, sliced
1 coriander, sliced
1/4 cup mint leaves

Spicy dressing

2 tablespoons light soy sauce
2 teaspoons brown sugar
1/2 teaspoon sea salt
1 tablespoon lime juice
1 tablespoon vinegar
10 green and red hot chilies, sliced

1. To prepare spicy dressing: combine light soy sauce, brown sugar, salt, lime juice and vinegar in a mixing bowl and stir until sugar is completely dissolved. Add hot chilies and put aside.
2. Wash eggplants, grill over high heat until cooked through and tender. Remove burnt skin and cut into 1 1/2" pieces. Arrange nicely on a serving plate.
3. Mash soft tofu into small pieces. Deep-fry in hot oil, using high heat at the beginning then reduce to medium heat. Fry until no bubbles remain and the tofu is golden crispy. Remove and drain.
4. In a mixing bowl, combine shallots, spring onions, coriander and spicy dressing together. Add mint leaves and toss well. Spoon over grilled eggplants and sprinkle crisp-fried tofu over the top. Serve immediately.

(Serves 2)

Use high heat to grill the eggplant so that its flesh will be done and tender. To cook the eggplant in a microwave oven: clean, halve crosswise and dip in water. Arrange on a plate and cover with plastic wrap. Put in a microwave oven and cook for 3 minutes, using medium-high heat. When done, take out and soak in a bowl of water for a few minutes before peeling off the skin.

Crispy Water Morning Glory with Roasted Chili Dressing

(yum phak-boong krob)

- 4 cups vegetable oil
- 2 bunches water morning glory, cut into 2" sections
- 1 bunch ivy gourd, leaves only
- 1 red onion, thinly sliced

The batter

- 1 egg
- 1 cup water
- 1/2 cup tempura flour
- 1/4 cup all purpose flour
- 1/4 cup rice flour
- 1 teaspoon baking powder

Roasted chili dressing

- 1 tablespoon vegetarian roasted chili paste
- 1 tablespoon light soy sauce
- 1 1/2 tablespoons lime juice
- 1/2 teaspoon sugar
- 9 hot chilies, crushed

1. To prepare the dressing: Combine roasted chili paste, light soy sauce, lime juice and sugar in a sauce bowl, stir until sugar has all dissolved. Taste and adjust to your liking. Add chilies, stir to mix well. Put aside.
2. To prepare the batter: In a mixing bowl, whisk egg with water until fluffy. Store in a freezer until icy cold. Take out of the freezer and add tempura flour, all purpose flour, rice flour and baking powder. With a whisk, combine the mixture to obtain a smooth and slightly thick batter.
3. Place a frying pan of oil over medium heat. When the oil is very hot, dip water morning glory in the batter and deep-fry until crispy and lightly golden. Remove and drain. Deep-fry ivy gourd and red onion in the same way. Continue until finished.
4. Arrange crisp-fried vegetables on a serving dish, spoon the roasted chili dressing over just before serving. Toss lightly and serve at once.

(Serves 2-3)

Select water morning glory only plump stems and freshly green leaves. Dip in the icy cold batter and deep-fry until all crispy. Toss the crisp vegetables with the dressing and serve immediately.

Vegetarian Crispy Shrimp Flake with Spicy Green Mango Salad

(yum ma-muang kub kung-foo je)

2 teaspoons unbleached sugar
2 tablespoons light soy sauce
2 1/2 tablespoons lime juice
1/4 cup shallots, sliced thinly
2 tablespoons sliced hot chilies
1 green mango, shredded
1/2 cup fried peanut, shelled
1/2 cup fried cashew nut
Fresh vegetables: Chinese cabbage, coriander, spring onion, cucumber, green ork leaves and sliced carrot

Vegetarian crispy shrimp flake

1 piece (240 grams) hard white tofu
1/2 cup breadcrumb
1/2 teaspoon sea salt
1/2 teaspoon pepper
2 tablespoons *mee kueng* flour
4 cups vegetable oil

1. To make shrimp flake: In a mixing bowl, mash tofu into small pieces. Add breadcrumb, salt, pepper and *mee kueng* flour toss well. The mixture should be slightly moist. Place a wok of oil over medium heat. When the oil is hot, deep-fry the mixture until golden and crispy, remove and drain.
2. To make spicy green mango salad: Mix sugar, light soy sauce and lime juice in another bowl, stir until sugar is completely dissolved. Add shallots, hot chilies and green mango. Mix well.
3. Arrange crispy shrimp flake on a serving dish, followed by peanut and cashew nut. Serve separately with spicy green mango salad. Alternatively, toss the shrimp flake with mango salad and serve immediately. Enjoy with fresh vegetables.

(Serves 2)

Both locally-produced and imported *mee kueng* flour are available. The one imported from China is more popular. It has off-white color, is sticky when touched and sold at an affordable price. While those imported from Australia are more expensive, darker in color but not sticky. Keep the flour in a sealed packet at a room temperature to prevent from moisture.

Vegetarian Salted Fish Salad

(yum plaa-khem je)

- 2 tubes (220 grams each) plain tube tofu
- 1/4 cup light soy sauce
- 1 tablespoon seasoning sauce
- 2 tablespoons vegetable oil
- 1 red shallot, thinly sliced crosswise
- 1 tablespoon hot chilies, sliced
- 1-2 wedges lime
- coriander for garnish

1. To make vegetarian salted fish: Put the tofu in a freezer until completely frozen (freezing overnight is recommended). Bring the frozen tofu out of a freezer, thaw and cut into halves. Softly press the tofu to get rid of the liquid as much as possible. When only the solid tofu remains, put into a mixing bowl, marinate with light soy sauce and seasoning sauce for hours.
2. Place a shallow pan over medium heat until it is slightly hot. Pour in oil and wait until the oil is hot. Fry marinated tofu until done and golden on both sides. Remove and arrange on a serving plate.
3. Sprinkle sliced red shallot and hot chilies on top and place lime wedges on the side, garnish with coriander before serving.

(Serves 2)

Plain tube tofu, a soft tofu available in a clear plastic tube, sometimes is called soup tofu or hygienic tofu. Buy tofu with its shelf life not exceed 7 days from the manufacturing date.

Thai Eggplant Salad

(yum ma-kheu-pror)

6 (40-50 grams each) young Thai eggplants
12 sheets (size 1"x2 1/2") nori seaweed, brushed with sesame oil and grilled
2 tablespoons white sesame seeds, roasted and lightly cracked
1/4 teaspoon sea salt
3 tablespoons shallots, thinly sliced
2 tablespoons lemongrass, diagonally sliced
1/4 cup mint leaves

Spicy dressing

15 green and red hot chilies
11 cloves Thai garlic, peeled
1 teaspoon dark fermented soybean
3 tablespoons light soy sauce
1 tablespoon brown sugar
2 1/2 tablespoons lime juice
1/8 teaspoon sea salt
1 tablespoon green and red hot chilies, sliced

1. To make spicy dressing: In a mortar, pound hot chilies and garlic coarsely, add dark fermented soybean and pound well. Dip out into a sauce bowl and season with light soy sauce, brown sugar, lime juice and salt. Stir until dissolved, add sliced chilies and put aside.
2. Wash eggplants, trim off stems and slice into pieces (Do not slice too thin as the eggplants will not be crisp). Soak in a bowl of lightly salted water to prevent from discoloration.
3. Tear nori seaweed into small pieces and put into another bowl, add sesame seeds and salt, toss well.
4. Drain the eggplants and put into a mixing bowl. Followed by sliced shallots, lemongrass, spicy dressing and mint leaves. Toss lightly to combine. Arrange the salad on a serving dish and top with salted sesame-seaweed. Serve at once.

(Serves 4)

Thai eggplant has sweet and crisp white flesh with pale yellow seeds. Always soak sliced eggplant in lightly salted water to prevent from discoloration. Select young eggplants with light green stems, cut into thick slices in order to obtain their crisp texture.

Spicy Vegetables Salad

(yum-yai phak)

- 1 cup unbleached mung bean noodles, soaked until tender and cut into short sections
- 2 teaspoons light soy sauce
- 2-3 tablespoons water, 1 teaspoon olive oil
- 50 grams carrot, thinly sliced lengthwise
- 50 grams Chinese radish, thinly sliced lengthwise
- 50 grams cucumber, seeded and thinly sliced lengthwise
- 1/4 cup dried bean curd skin, soaked, blanched and cut into pieces
- 1/4 cup mint leaves
- 1/4 cup coriander leaves
- 1/2 each red and yellow spur chilies, thinly sliced
- 2 pieces deep-fried dried bean curd skin
- 2 tablespoons cashew nut, fried and lightly cracked
- coriander for garnish

Spicy dressing

- 1/2 red spur chili, sliced
- 1 tablespoon Thai garlic, peeled
- 1 tablespoon coriander root, sliced
- 1 bulb pickled garlic, separated into cloves
- 2 tablespoons light soy sauce
- 1 teaspoon seasoning sauce
- 3 tablespoons brown sugar
- 3 tablespoons lime juice
- 1 tablespoon vinegar, 1/4 teaspoon sea salt

1. To make spicy dressing: Pound chili, garlic, coriander root and pickled garlic finely. Stir in light soy sauce, seasoning sauce, brown sugar, lime juice, vinegar and salt, adjust the taste to your liking.
2. In a small pot, put in mung bean noodles, light soy sauce, water and olive oil. Place over low heat and stir continuously until the noodles are done and tender. Remove from the heat and transfer to a mixing bowl. Add the dressing, toss well. When it is cool down, add carrot, Chinese radish, cucumber and blanched bean curd skin, toss to combine. Add mint leaves, coriander leaves and chilies (keep some for topping). Tossing again.
3. Dip out into a serving dish and top with fried bean curd skin, mint leaves, coriander leaves, chilies and fried cashew nut. Garnish with coriander and serve immediately.

(Serves 2)

Fresh cucumber provides low energy and is very refreshing. It contains a lot of juice which helps freshen up the skin. Select small cucumbers with white strips on the green skin. The flesh is thick and crispy sweet with small amount of seeds. Tiny cucumbers are those which are too young, have lots of slime and a bitter taste.

Vegetarian Tuna and Herbs Salad

(yum sa-moon-phrai plaa tuna je)

1 cup vegetarian tuna
1/4 cup shallot, sliced thinly
1/4 cup young ginger, shredded
1/4 cup lemongrass, sliced thinly
1/4 cup young galangal, shredded
1/4 cup wild ginger, shredded
4-5 kaffir lime leaves, shredded
1/4 cup mint leaves
iceberg lettuce and lemon wedge for garnish

Spicy dressing

2 tablespoons light soy sauce
2 tablespoons lime juice
1/4 teaspoon sea salt
1/2 teaspoon sugar
7 hot chilies, sliced

1. To make spicy dressing: In a sauce bowl, combine light soy sauce, lime juice, salt and sugar. Stir until all dissolved. Add hot chilies and stir lightly.
2. In a mixing bowl, put in vegetarian tuna, shallot, ginger, lemongrass, galangal and wild ginger. Spoon the dressing over and toss to combine. Add kaffir lime leaves and mint leaves, toss lightly.
3. Transfer to serving dish, garnish with iceberg lettuce and lemon wedge. Serve at once.

(Serves 4)

Vegetarian tuna is made from textured vegetable protein (TVP), seasoned to tastes like the real tuna. It is available both in can and in packet, and can be found in many supermarkets during the Vegetarian festival. When off-season, you can find it from grocery shops at soi Isaranuphap, Yaowarat (Chinatown) and those vegetarian supermarkets.

Spicy Green Mango Salad with Mushroom Tempura

(yum ma-muang tempura hed)

1/2 cup green mango, shredded
1/2 cup carrot, shredded
1/2 cup red cabbage, shredded
1/4 cup pea sprouts
angel mushroom tempura as desired

Angel mushroom tempura

200 grams angel mushrooms, torn
1/2 cup tempura flour
1/2 cup icy cold clear lime liquid
1 tablespoon white sesame seeds
1/4 teaspoon sea salt
1/4 teaspoon ground black pepper
3 cups vegetable oil

Spicy dressing (1/2 cup)

7 green and red hot chilies, coarsely chopped
2 dried hot chilies, pounded
1 tablespoon+1 teaspoon palm sugar
3 tablespoons light soy sauce
2 tablespoons lime juice
2 tablespoons tamarind juice
2 tablespoons coconut cream
3 tablespoons roasted peanut, ground

1. To prepare mushroom tempura: Air-dry angel mushrooms until they are slightly dry. Mix tempura flour with clear lime liquid in a mixing bowl. Add white sesame seeds and season with salt and black pepper. Dip angel mushrooms into the batter and deep-fry in hot oil over medium heat until golden and crispy. Remove and drain.
2. To prepare spicy dressing: Combine all ingredients together. Add ground peanut just before serving.
3. Put all kinds of vegetables in a refrigerator until icy cold. To serve, arrange them attractively on a serving dish and serve with spicy dressing and mushroom tempura.

(Serves 2)

With a mouthwatering taste of sour, salty and sweet from the dressing, you can also enjoy the crunchiness from freshly roasted peanut and mushroom tempura. Select angel mushrooms that are fresh and not soggy. Tear into pieces and leave to dry slightly before dipping in the cold tempura batter and deep-frying. The mushrooms will be crispy and not oily after cooked.

Country-Style TVP Salad

(laab protein ka-sed)

- 1 piece (280 grams) soft tofu
- 1 cup fresh black ear mushrooms, sliced
- 1/2 cup dried Shanghai noodles, soaked and cut into small pieces
- 8 straw mushrooms, coarsely chopped
- 1/2 cup textured vegetable protein (TVP), soaked until tender, squeezed and finely chopped
- 3 tablespoons light soy sauce
- 1 tablespoon roasted dried hot chili, ground
- 3 tablespoons lime juice
- 1/4 teaspoon sea salt
- 1 tablespoon ground roasted rice
- 2 tablespoons shallot, thinly sliced
- 1 spring onion, sliced
- 1 saw-leaves coriander, sliced
- 1/4 cup mint leaves
- mint sprig for garnish
- Fresh vegetables: iceberg lettuce, Chinese cabbage, yard-long bean, sweet basil, mint, etc.

1. Add small amount of salt in a pot of water and bring to the boil over high heat. Add tofu and boil until done and floated to the surface. The tofu will have a firm texture. Transfer boiled tofu to a mixing bowl, mash into small pieces. Dry-fry in a pan over low heat until totally dry, fragrant and lightly golden. Put aside.
2. In another pan, dry-fry black ear mushrooms and Shanghai noodles over low heat until done. Turn off the heat and transfer to a mixing bowl. In a new pan, dry-fry straw mushrooms and TVP, one at a time, until fragrant and done. Remove and transfer to the same mixing bowl. Leave to cool.
3. Pour light soy sauce over cooked mushrooms, add fried tofu, ground chili, lime juice and salt. Toss to mix well. Add ground rice, shallot, spring onion and saw-leaves coriander. Tossing again and top with mint leaves.
4. Spoon onto iceberg lettuce leaf and garnish with mint sprig before serving. Enjoy with fresh vegetables.

(Serves 4-6)

Shanghai noodles is made from mung bean flour, available both fresh and dried types. Dried noodles are clearer and thinner, and must be soaked before cooking. Fresh noodles come in the form of light green rolls with a soft and chewy texture and thicker sheets.

Spicy Mushrooms Salad

(laab hed saam yaang)

- 5 eryngii mushrooms
- 15 straw mushrooms
- 20 small fresh shiitake mushrooms
- 2 tablespoons light soy sauce
- 2 teaspoons roasted dried hot chili, ground
- 1/4 teaspoon sea salt
- 1 1/2 tablespoons lime juice
- 1 tablespoon ground roasted rice
- 1/4 cup shallot thinly sliced
- 1 spring onion, sliced
- 1 saw-leaves coriander, sliced
- 1/4 cup mint leaves

Fresh vegetables: sweet basil leaves, mint, Chinese cabbage, etc.

1. With a cloth, wipe out dirt from the mushrooms and trim off hard stalks. Put into a pot and place over medium heat. Dry-fry until all are dried and heated through. Remove from the heat. Diagonally slice eryngii mushrooms and cut straw mushrooms into quarters. Put all mushrooms into a mixing bowl.
2. Add light soy sauce into the bowl, followed by ground chili, salt and lime juice. Toss to mix well. Add ground rice, shallot, spring onion, saw-leaves coriander and mint leaves, toss again. The salad should have a combination of spicy, sour, salty and sweet.
3. Dip out into a serving dish and enjoy with fresh vegetables.

(Serves 4)

Roasted rice will be fragrant, crisp and easy to be ground if you use uncooked sticky rice. Wash the rice, dry-fry in a pan over low heat until cooked and golden brown. The color will be lighter when ground.

Spicy TVP Salad

(nam-tok protein ka-sed)

- 3 cups vegetable oil
- 3 large pieces dark textured vegetable protein (TVP)
- 5 tablespoons light soy sauce
- 1 teaspoon palm sugar
- 1/2 teaspoon pepper
- 1 1/2 teaspoons sweet dark soy sauce
- 1 teaspoon roasted dried hot chili, ground
- 1 1/2 tablespoons lime juice
- 1/4 cup thinly sliced shallot
- 1 teaspoon ground roasted rice
- 1/4 cup saw-leaves coriander, sliced
- 1/2 cup mint leaves
- Fresh vegetables: lettuce, yard-long bean, cucumber, sliced carrot, etc.

1. Pre-heat a wok of oil over medium heat until the oil is hot. Fry TVP until done. Remove from the oil and soak in hot water until tender. Squeeze to dry and put into a bowl. Add 2 tablespoons of light soy sauce, palm sugar, pepper and sweet dark soy sauce. Marinate for at least 1 hour.
2. Grill marinated TVP over moderate heat until fragrant and heated through. Slice thinly and put into a mixing bowl. Add the remaining light soy sauce, ground chili and lime juice. Toss to combine. Add shallot, roasted rice, saw-leaves coriander and mint leaves. Tossing again.
3. Ladle onto a serving dish and serve with fresh vegetables.

(Serves 2-3)

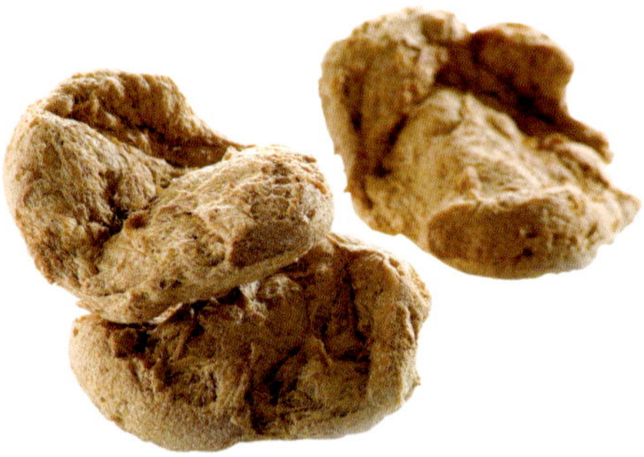

Textured vegetable protein (TVP) usually has a nutty or oily smell. Fry and soak or boil until tender can help reduce its unpleasant odor. Always squeeze them until completely dry before mixing with other ingredients so that they can absorb the seasonings quite well.

Tempeh with Spicy Mushrooms and Green Mango

(tempeh plah ma-muang kub hed)

- 1 piece (150 grams) tempeh
- 2 teaspoons light soy sauce
- 1/2 teaspoon sugar
- 50 grams seasoned hiratake mushrooms
- 1 1/2 cups green mango, shredded
- 1/2 cup lemongrass, thinly sliced
- 4 shallots, thinly sliced
- 1 tablespoon hot chilies, sliced
- 1/4 cup mint leaves
- 1 tablespoon kaffir lime leaves, shredded
- green ork lettuce for lining

Roasted chili paste (3 tablespoons)

- 9 dried red spur chilies, roasted
- 1/4 cup Thai garlic, roasted
- 3 shallots, roasted
- 2 teaspoons dark fermented soybean

Spicy dressing

- 2 tablespoons roasted chili paste
- 2 tablespoons light soy sauce
- 1 tablespoon lime juice
- 2 teaspoons sugar

1. To prepare roasted chili paste: Finely pound dried chilies, garlic and shallots together. Add fermented soybean and pound well. Put aside.
2. To prepare the dressing: Combine roasted chili paste, light soy sauce, lime juice and sugar together. Stir until sugar has all dissolved. (Keep the remaining roasted chili paste in a refrigerator).
3. Cut tempeh into thin slices and grill in the pan until is slightly golden. Put aside.
4. To prepare seasoned hiratake mushrooms: Combine light soy sauce and sugar in a sauce dish, stir to dissolve. Dry-fry mushrooms over medium heat until cooked through. Add in light soy sauce mixture and toss well. Remove from the heat and put aside.
5. In a mixing bowl, put in shredded green mango, lemongrass, shallots and hot chilies. Toss to combine. Add spicy dressing, seasoned mushrooms and grilled tempeh. Toss to mix well. Add mint leaves and toss again lightly.
6. Spoon onto a plate lined with green ork lettuce, sprinkle shredded kaffir lime leaves on top before serving.

(Serves 2)

Either normal tempeh or tempeh with sesame seeds can be used in this recipe. It can be found in selected supermarkets and many health food stores. Look for manufacturing date and expiry date shown on its label before picking from the shelf. It is recommended to store tempeh refrigerated at all times.

Garden Salad with Tri-Color Dressings

(salad phak kub nam salad saam see)

2-3 leaves iceberg lettuce, torn
4 leaves lettuce, torn
1/2 cup watercress, leaves only
2 tomatoes, sliced crosswise
2 onions, sliced into rings
3 cucumbers, sliced diagonally
1/2 cup each shredded carrot and red cabbage
1/2 cup each boiled red bean and boiled brown job's tear
1/2 cup water chestnut, boiled and peeled
1/2 cup hulled mung bean, steamed
1/2 cup pumpkin, peeled cut into pieces and steamed
1/2 cup boiled corn kernels

Basic salad dressing

1/2 cup rice vinegar
2 tablespoons mustard cream
1 tablespoon pepper, 1 tablespoon sea salt
1/2 cup olive oil
2 cans (388 grams each) sweet condensed milk
1 can (405 grams) evaporated milk
1 bottle (450 grams) fresh milk
1/3 cup lime juice
1 cup pumpkin, peeled, cut into pieces and steamed
1 (180 grams) carrot, peeled, cut into small cubes and boiled
1 (180 grams) beetroot, peeled, cut into small cubes and boiled

1. Attractively arrange iceberg lettuce, lettuce, watercress, tomatoes, onions, cucumbers, carrot and red cabbage on a serving dish and keep refrigerated until served.
2. To prepare the salad dressing: In a blender, put in vinegar, mustard, pepper and salt, blend at a medium speed. Gradually add olive oil, a little at a time, until finished. Blend until the mixture becomes light cream color. Add all milk and blend well. Add lime juice, continue blending until it is thick and creamy. Pour into a bowl and keep refrigerated.
3. Put 2 cups of the salad dressing into a new blender, add steamed pumpkin and blend well at a medium speed. Transfer to a jar or a closed container. Repeat the same process with carrot and beetroot.
4. Arrange cooked red bean, job's tear, water chestnut, mung bean, pumpkin and corn kernels on the bed of prepared green salad in step 1. Spoon the dressing of your choice over or serve separately as preferred.

(Serves 4-5)

Mustard is an emulsifier used to help combine liquid ingredients and oil together. Mustard cream composes of powdered mustard, vinegar, salt and spices, whereas mustard powder has to be mixed with the same amount of water before used.

Garden Salad with Sesame Oil Dressing

(salad phak nam-mun-ngaa)

- 1/4 cup sweet potato, cut into pieces and boiled
- 1/4 cup *khai* potato, cut into pieces and boiled
- 1/4 cup red potato, cut into pieces and boiled
- 3 tablespoons boiled corn kernels
- 1/4 piece (70 grams) soft tofu, cut into cubes and fried until just golden
- 3 tablespoons sesame oil dressing
- 1 cup mixed salad leaves
- 1 tablespoon roasted peanut, cracked

Sesame oil dressing (3/4 cup)

- 1/2 cup tamarind juice
- 1/4 cup+1 tablespoon sugar
- 1/2 teaspoon sea salt
- 2 tablespoons olive oil
- 1 teaspoon sesame oil
- 2 tablespoons roasted black sesame seeds, lightly cracked

1. To prepare the dressing: combine tamarind juice, sugar and salt together, stir until all dissolved. Gradually add olive oil and sesame oil, stir to blend well. Add black sesame seeds, stirring again to combine.
2. In a mixing bowl, put in all potatoes, corn kernels and fried tofu. Toss well with sesame oil dressing, spoon onto a bed of mixed salad leaves in a serving dish and sprinkle roasted peanut on top. Serve immediately.

(Serves 2)

Always use roasted sesame oil to prepare the dressing as it gives stronger aroma than the ordinary one but is darker in color. Good roasted sesame oil must be thick and is quite expensive. It is available both locally produced and imported ones. Sesame oil contains high unsaturated fat which helps reduce blood cholesterol, prevent harden arterial walls and heart disease.

Savory Phuket Salad

(salad phak phuket)

2 lettuce plants
1 yam bean, julienne
1 large cucumber, slice the flesh into strips
1 cup blanched water morning glory
1 cup blanched bean sprouts
1 cup yellow tofu, sliced and crisp-fried
3 cups Phuket rice vermicelli (mee hoon), crisp-fried
2 soft boiled eggs

Spicy dressing

100 grams dried red spur chilies, seeded and soaked until tender
100 grams Thai garlic, peeled
500 grams sugar
6 cups water
1/2 cup tamarind juice
1 tablespoon sea salt
1/4 cup vinegar

1. To make spicy dressing: In a mortar, thoroughly pound dried chilies and garlic. Dip out into a pot and mix with sugar, water, tamarind juice and salt. Place the pot over medium heat and cook until slightly thickened. Add vinegar, cook until boiling. Turn off the heat. The dressing should be a bit sweet.
2. Tear lettuce leaves into pieces. Arrange yam bean, large cucumber, water morning glory, bean sprouts and fried tofu attractively on a serving dish. Break fried Phuket rice vermicelli into pieces and place on top. Spoon the dressing over and place boiled eggs on the side. Serve at once.

(Serves 4)

Phuket salad or *Hoo Chae*, as it is called locally, is served as a light lunch or snack. It is also served during the Vegetarian festival. Normal rice vermicelli, a good substitution for Phuket rice vermicelli *(mee hoon)*, is slightly thinner. Prepare the dressing in bulk and keep refrigerated, pour over fresh salad leaves and fried tofu whenever desired.

Green Papaya Salad

(som-tum ma-la-kor)

- 2 cups green papaya, shredded (*khaek nuan* variety is preferred)
- 1/2 cup shredded carrot
- Fresh vegetables: cabbage and yard-long bean

Dried chili dressing

- 6 dried hot chilies
- 4 cloves Thai garlic, peeled
- 1 pod yard-long bean, cut into 1" sections
- 2 tablespoons roasted peanut
- 1 1/2 teaspoons palm sugar
- 1 cherry tomato
- 1 tablespoon dark fermented soybean with its liquid
- 1 tablespoon boiled tamarind juice
- 1 tablespoon lime juice
- 1/2 teaspoon light soy sauce, a dash of salt

Fresh chili dressing

- 5 fresh green and red hot chilies
- 5 cloves Thai garlic, peeled
- 1 pod yard-long bean, cut into 1" sections
- 2 tablespoons roasted peanut
- 1 1/2 teaspoon palm sugar
- 1 cherry tomato, 2 ripe hog plums
- 1 1/2 tablespoons dark fermented soybean with its liquid
- 1 teaspoon boiled tamarind juice
- 2 1/2 teaspoons lime juice
- a dash of salt

1. To prepare dried chili dressing: In a mortar, coarsely pound dried hot chilies. Add garlic and yard-long bean, lightly crushed. Add roasted peanut, crushed. Add in palm sugar, cut cherry tomato into pieces and put in. Followed by dark fermented soybean and its liquid, tamarind juice, lime juice, light soy sauce and salt. Pound and toss to mix well. Adjust the taste to your liking, the taste should be sour, salty and sweet. Add half of shredded green papaya and carrot. Pound and toss lightly to combine. Dip out into a serving dish and serve with fresh vegetables.
2. To prepare fresh chili dressing: Pound fresh hot chilies and garlic coarsely. Add yard-long bean and peanut, crushed lightly. Add palm sugar, slice cherry tomato and hog plums and put in. Followed by dark fermented soybean and its liquid, tamarind juice, lime juice and salt. Season to taste, it should be sour, salty and sweet. Pound and toss to combine. Add the remaining green papaya and carrot, pound and toss again. Enjoy with fresh vegetables.

(Serves 2)

Khaek nuan variety is a papaya consumed only when it is green as it has crisp and thick flesh with small amount of seeds.

Vegetarian Shrimp Paste Dip

(nam-phrik ka-pi)

- 3 Thai eggplants
- 1 piece Northern fermented soybean *(dried thua-nao)*, grilled until fragrant
- 9 cloves Thai garlic, peeled
- 5 cubes red fermented tofu, fried in small amount of oil until lightly golden (used instead of shrimp paste)
- 15 hot chilies
- 15 pea eggplants
- 3 tablespoons boiled water
- 1 1/2 teaspoons palm sugar
- 1/2 teaspoon sea salt
- 2 tablespoons lime juice
- hot chilies for garnish
- Fresh vegetables: cucumber, water morning glory, Chinese cabbage, yard-long bean, carrot and various kinds of eggplants
- Condiment: pan-fried shiitake mushrooms (page 160)

1. Wash Thai eggplants well, cut halves, soak in a bowl of lightly salted water to prevent from discolored. With a spoon, scoop out flesh and seeds, put aside.
2. Thoroughly pound fermented soybean and garlic with a mortar and a pestle. Add eggplant flesh and seeds and fermented tofu, pound well. Add hot chilies and pea eggplants, crushed lightly. Add in water and stir to mix well. Season to taste with palm sugar, salt and lime juice. Stir well.
3. Dip out into a serving bowl, garnish with hot chilies. Serve with fresh vegetables and condiment.

(Serves 4)

Good quality red fermented tofu is used in this recipe. Buy those with an aromatic smooth texture. Red fermented tofu wrapped in a piece of bamboo leaves is of the premium quality. It has stronger aroma, quite expensive and can be found only in selected grocery shops. Fry the tofu in small amount of oil until lightly golden in order to enhance its fragrance.

Roasted Chili Paste with Tofu

(nam-phrik-phao tao-hoo)

- 1 piece (200 grams) semi-hard white tofu, mashed
- 1/2 cup vegetable oil
- 1/2 cup sliced shallot
- 1/4 cup Thai garlic, peel and slice thinly
- 15 dried red spur chilies, dry-fried or roasted
- 1 cube red fermented tofu, about 1" size
- 2 tablespoons light soy sauce
- 1 tablespoon+1 teaspoon palm sugar
- 3 tablespoons tamarind juice
- 1/8 teaspoon sea salt

Fresh vegetables: carrot, cucumber, red bell pepper and Chinese celery

1. Fry tofu in hot oil over medium heat until golden. Remove and drain off excess oil (Do not over-fry or the tofu will become hard). Fry sliced shallot and garlic, one at a time, until golden crispy. Remove and drain as well.
2. In a mortar, pound dried red spur chilies, fried shallot and fried garlic until fine. Add red fermented tofu and continue pounding well. Add fried tofu and pound to combine. Transfer to a pan and sauté with 1 tablespoon of the oil reserved from fried shallot. Cook over medium heat until fragrant. Season to taste with light soy sauce, palm sugar, tamarind juice and salt. The taste should have a combination of sour, sweet, salty and slightly hot. Turn off the heat.
3. Dip out into a serving dish and serve with fresh vegetables.

(Serves 4)

Semi-hard white tofu is yellowish white with slightly strong smell of bean than soft tofu. The texture is hard and it can be kept for 1-2 week(s) by soaking with cold-boiled water in a bowl then put in a refrigerator.

Tangy Tomato Dip

(nam-phrik-ong khai)

19 roasted dried hot chilies
25 cloves Thai garlic, peeled
5 shallots, sliced
1 piece Northern fermented soybean *(dried thua-nao)*, grilled until fragrant
1 1/2 cups tangy tomatoes
3 tablespoons vegetable oil
1 egg
1 cup water or vegetable stock (version 1 page 13)
1/4 teaspoon sea salt
2 tablespoons light soy sauce
1 tablespoon sugar
2 tablespoons tasty shredded mushroom (page 174)
Fresh vegetables: Chinese cabbage, green ork leaves, cucumber, yard-long bean, winged bean, okra, carrot and various kinds of eggplants

1. In a mortar, pound dried chilies, garlic and shallots to a fine paste. Add fermented soybean and pound well. Add tangy tomatoes, pound and crush lightly.
2. Place a pan over medium heat and add 2 tablespoons of oil. When the oil is hot, sauté chili mixture until fragrant. Turn to low heat and move the mixture to the side of the pan. Add the remaining oil and break in an egg. Toss the chili mixture with egg and add water or stock. Season to taste with salt, light soy sauce and sugar. Cook until the sauce reduces and tomatoes are done and tender. Taste for a perfect balance of spicy, sour and salty. Turn off the heat.
3. Ladle into a serving bowl and top with tasty shredded mushroom. Enjoy with fresh vegetables and steamed sticky rice.

(Serves 4)

Tangy tomato is the smallest variety in the tomato family. Its fruits grow in cluster with a thin reddish-orange skin when ripe. Its taste is sourer than any other varieties. Select only fresh fruits with firm skin, green stalk and no sign of bruises.

Green Tamarind Dip

(nam-phrik ma-khaam on)

- 50 grams green tamarind
- 3 tablespoons vegetarian shrimp paste
- 4 pickled Chinese olives, pitted
- 1/4 cup roasted cashew nut, coarsely cracked
- 10 hot chilies
- 1/4 cup soup seaweed, grilled until fragrant and torn into small pieces
- 1 tablespoon dark fermented soybean
- 2 tablespoons boiled water or vegetable stock (version 1 page 13)
- 1 tablespoon palm sugar
- 1/2 tablespoon light soy sauce
- 1/2 tablespoon seasoning sauce
- red hot chilies for garnish
- Vegetable tempura: long eggplant, acacia tips, chayote tips, water morning glory, etc.
- Fresh vegetables: yard-long bean, white turmeric, lead tree tips, eggplants, etc.
- banana leaf for wrapping

1. Wash green tamarind, remove all the dust. Drain, cut into small pieces and put aside.
2. Wrap vegetarian shrimp paste in banana leaf and char-grill until fragrant.
3. In a mortar, thoroughly pound shrimp paste and pickled Chinese olives. Add cashew nut and tamarind, pound to fine paste. Add hot chilies, seaweed and fermented soybean, pound lightly. Stir in water or stock and season to your liking with palm sugar, light soy sauce and seasoning sauce. Stir to combine.
4. Ladle into a serving bowl and garnish with hot chilies. Serve with vegetable tempura and fresh vegetables.

(Serves 4)

Green tamarind has a sour and a bit of astringent taste. Its season is during late October to early November. Buy those with thick seedless pods and sour flesh. Too young tamarind will have flat pods, slightly sourness and stronger astringent taste. Green tamarind contains a lot of vitamin A which helps soothing sore throat.

Crunchy Green Mango Dip

(nam-phrik ma-muang)

- 1/3 cup roasted cashew nut
- 25 cloves Thai garlic, peeled
- 3 shallots, sliced
- 3 tablespoons grilled vegetarian shrimp paste or yellow fermented tofu
- 3 tablespoons dark fermented soybean
- 3 pickled Chinese olives, pitted
- 17 green and red hot chilies
- 1 (250 grams) green *nam dok mai* mango, shredded
- 1 tablespoon palm sugar
- 1/3 cup straw mushrooms, oyster mushrooms and angel mushrooms, dry-fried and chopped
- 3 tablespoons boiled water or vegetable stock (version 1 page 13)
- 1/2 piece (10 grams) soup seaweed, grilled until fragrant and torn into small pieces

Fresh vegetables: yard-long bean, okra, white turmeric, lead tree tips, wild bitter gourd, eggplants, etc.

1. In a mortar, pound cashew nut finely. Add garlic, shallots and vegetarian shrimp paste, pound to fine paste. Add dark fermented soybean and pickled Chinese olives. Continue pounding to a smooth paste. Add chilies, pound coarsely. Add shredded mango (reserve some for topping), pound lightly. Add palm sugar, chopped mushrooms, water or stock and grilled seaweed. Pound and toss to mix well.
2. Dip out into a serving bowl and top with shredded green mango. Serve with fresh vegetables.

(Serves 4-6)

Nam dok mai variety is used in this recipe due to its sharp sourness. Younger fruit with a soft seed and white flesh has a sharp sour taste while the nearly-ripe fruit is quite sweet with a dash of sour. Vegetarian shrimp paste, dark fermented soybean and pickled Chinese olive are a good replacement for shrimp paste as they provide the flavor, color and texture to the dip the same as the real one does.

Aromatic Chili Dip

(nam-phrik taa-daeng)

- 10 dried red spur chilies
- 15 dried red hot chilies
- 8 shallots, sliced
- 1/2 cup Thai garlic, peeled
- 1 1/2 tablespoons vegetarian shrimp paste
- 1/4 cup+1 tablespoon dark fermented soybean with its liquid
- 1/4 cup water
- 2 tablespoons white sesame seeds, finely pounded
- 2 tablespoons black sesame seeds, finely pounded
- 1 tablespoon+1 teaspoon palm sugar
- 3 tablespoons boiled tamarind juice
- 1 tablespoon seasoning sauce
- 1 tablespoon light soy sauce
- Fresh vegetables: wild bitter gourd, lead tree tips, yard-long bean, eggplants, etc.
- Blanched vegetables: bamboo shoot, etc.
- banana leaf for wrapping

1. Dry-fry or roast chilies over low heat until puff and crisp. Remove from the heat and put aside. Dry-fry shallots and garlic until slightly blackened. Wrap shrimp paste in a banana leaf and grill over medium heat until fragrant.
2. Boil dark fermented soybean with its liquid and water over moderate heat until boiling. Turn off the heat and leave to cool completely.
3. In a mortar, thoroughly pound both kinds of chilies. Add shallots, garlic, shrimp paste and cooked fermented soybean, pound well after each adding. Stir in liquid from fermented soybean. Add white and black sesame seeds, palm sugar, tamarind juice, seasoning sauce and light soy sauce, pound and toss lightly to mix well. Taste and adjust to you liking.
4. Transfer to a serving bowl. Best when serve with assorted vegetables and hot steamed rice or sticky rice.

(Serves 4)

This kind of chili dip has a perfect balance of sour, salty and sweet. Both dried red spur chilies and hot chilies are used in this recipe. Select dried chilies with thin skin; it can be easily pounded to a fine powder. For those with a shiny skin, they will be flaky rather powdery when being pounded.

Hog Plum Dip

(nam-phrik ma-kok-paa)

- 7 ripe hog plums
- 2 tablespoons vegetarian shrimp paste
- 15 large size red hot chilies
- 2 green bell chilies, sliced
- 5 shallots, sliced
- 15 cloves Thai garlic, peeled
- 7 straw mushrooms, chopped
- 30 grams angel mushrooms, chopped
- 30 grams oyster mushrooms, chopped
- 1 teaspoon sea salt
- 2 tablespoons roasted cashew nut
- 1 tablespoon dark fermented soybean
- 1 tablespoon seasoning sauce
- 1 teaspoon light soy sauce
- 1/2 piece (10 grams) soup seaweed, grilled until fragrant and torn into small pieces

Fresh vegetables: winged bean, yard-long bean, wild bitter gourd, white turmeric, eggplants, etc.

Blanched vegetables: flowering cabbage

banana leaf for wrapping

1. Wrap hog plums in a double-layer of banana leaf. Char-grill over moderate heat until done and fragrant, leave to cool. Thinly slice and put aside. Wrap vegetarian shrimp paste with banana leaf and grilled until fragrant, put aside.
2. Dry-fry or roast hot chilies, bell chilies, shallots and garlic together over medium heat until cooked through. Remove and put aside.
3. Dry-fry all mushrooms with salt over medium heat until done.
4. Pound chilies with shallots and garlic coarsely. Add cashew nut and pound to combine. Add mushrooms, hog plums and shrimp paste. Pound to mix well. Season with dark fermented soybean, seasoning sauce and light soy sauce. Add seaweed, pound and toss to combine.
5. Dip out into a serving dish and serve with assorted vegetables.

(Serves 4)

Hog plum is used to add sourness and its unique aroma to many dishes. Its season is in winter. Ripe fruit has a combination of sour and astringent flavor with a sweetness after-taste. Select those with a lot of yellow dots and just ripe; its flesh will be soft but not mushy and has a strong aroma.

Pickled Chinese Olive Dip

(nam-phrik num-leab)

- 1 tablespoon Thai garlic, peeled and sliced
- 6 pickled Chinese olives, pitted
- 1 red spur chili, sliced
- 2 yellow spur chilies, sliced
- 7 hot chilies
- 2 *ma euk* (a kind of eggplant), hair removed and thinly sliced
- 1/4 cup hard white tofu, mashed and dry-fried until golden
- 3 tablespoons light soy sauce
- 2 1/2 tablespoons brown sugar
- 2 tablespoons lime juice
- 3/4 teaspoon sea salt
- hot chilies for garnish
- Fresh vegetables: winged bean, yard-long bean, cucumber, white turmeric, water morning glory, eggplants, etc.

1. In a mortar, pound garlic and pickled Chinese olives to a smooth paste. Add red and yellow spur chilies, pour coarsely. Add hot chilies and crush lightly. Add *ma euk* and cooked mashed tofu, pound lightly just to combine. Season well with light soy sauce, brown sugar, lime juice and salt. Taste and adjust to a balanced taste of sour, salty and sweet.
2. Ladle to a serving bowl and garnish with hot chilies before serving with fresh vegetables.

(Serves 2)

Pickled Chinese olive is a preserved olive in brine with a purplish black salty flesh and a unique fragrance. Those with seeds are available in many kinds of packaging i.e. in a can or in a bottle while pure pickled Chinese olive flesh is normally sold by weight.

Vegetarian Fermented Fish Dip

(lon plaa-raa je song-kreung)

- 1/4 cup+1 tablespoon vegetarian fermented fish
- 2 1/4 cups coconut cream
- 1 stem lemongrass, coarsely sliced
- 2-3 slices mature galangal
- 2 kaffir lime leaves, torn
- 5 shallots, sliced thinly
- 5 roots wild ginger, shredded
- 2 stems lemongrass, sliced thinly
- 2 tablespoons mature galangal, sliced thinly
- 1/2 piece (100 grams) hard white tofu, diced
- 2 pods yard-long bean, cut into 1.5 cm pieces
- 2 Thai eggplants, quartered
- 1/2 cup coconut shoot, cut into strips
- 6 straw mushrooms, halved and thinly sliced
- 1 teaspoon light soy sauce
- 1/2 teaspoon sea salt
- 1/2 teaspoon unbleached sugar
- 1 tablespoon kaffir lime leaves, shredded
- kaffir lime leaves and hot chilies for garnish
- Fresh vegetables: cucumber, yard-long bean, Chinese cabbage, carrot, eggplants, etc.

1. Boil vegetarian fermented fish with 1 cup of coconut cream in a pot over medium heat until boiling. Add lemongrass, galangal and kaffir lime leaves, boil for further 10 minutes. Turn off the heat, strain and reserve only the liquid.
2. In a new pot, combine the liquid prepared in step 1 with another cup of coconut cream and bring to the boil over medium heat. Add in shallots, wild ginger, lemongrass and galangal. Bring back to the boil and add tofu, yard-long bean, Thai eggplants, coconut shoot and straw mushrooms. When all vegetables are done, season well with light soy sauce, salt and sugar. Stir to mix well, add the remaining coconut cream and shredded kaffir lime leaves. Taste and adjust to your liking.
3. Transfer to a serving bowl, garnish with fresh kaffir lime leaves and hot chilies. Enjoy with fresh vegetables.

(Serves 4)

Vegetarian fermented fish is made from seasoned fermented soybean. It has a smooth texture with dark brown color and unique fragrance. Vegetarian fermented fish contains a lot of vitamin B12; it can be found in general vegetarian restaurants and can be stored at a room temperature for months.

Fermented Soybean Dip

(tao-jiaw lon)

- 1 cup white fermented soybean
- 1/2 cup coconut milk
- 5 coriander roots, pounded finely
- 1/2 piece (75 grams) hard white tofu, diced
- 7 straw mushrooms, chopped
- 50 grams chopped oyster mushrooms
- 50 grams enoki mushrooms, cut into 1" sections
- 5 shallots, thinly sliced
- 5 roots wild ginger, sliced crosswise
- 3 tablespoonspalm sugar
- 1/4 cup+2 tablespoons tamarind juice
- 1 tablespoon seasoning sauce
- 1 tablespoon light soy sauce
- 1/2 cup low-fat milk
- 1 green spur chili, sliced
- 1 red spur chili, sliced
- 3 green bell chilies, sliced
- 1 cup coconut cream
- fresh coriander leaves for garnish
- Fresh vegetables: white turmeric, stinky bean, lead tree tips, yard-long bean, eggplants, etc.

1. Wash fermented soybean twice to reduce its saltiness. Drain and pound finely. Put aside.
2. In a pot, bring coconut milk to a rolling boil over medium heat. Add coriander roots and pounded fermented soybean, stir well. Add tofu and all mushrooms, cook to boiling and mushrooms are cooked through. Add shallots and wild ginger, boil for a few minutes. Season with palm sugar, tamarind juice, seasoning sauce and light soy sauce. Stirring to combine. Add milk, stir again. Taste and adjust to a balanced taste of sweet, salty and sour. Add chilies and cook until done. Add coconut cream and turn off the heat.
3. Ladle into a serving dish and garnish with fresh coriander leaves. Enjoy with fresh vegetables. (Serves 6-8)

White fermented soybean is made by mixing soybeans with the mixture left from making the soy sauce. Add in brine and leave to ferment. The fermentation period of white fermented soybean is not as long as dark fermented one. It has full bean with a light yellow color.

Savory White Tofu Dip

(tao-hoo khua)

- 1/2 piece (75 grams) semi-hard white tofu
- 2 dried red spur chilies, seeded and soaked until tender
- 1 teaspoon mature galangal, finely sliced
- 2 tablespoons lemongrass, finely sliced
- 1/2 teaspoon kaffir lime rind, finely sliced
- 1/4 cup wild ginger, sliced
- 1 shallot, sliced
- 2 tablespoons dark fermented soybean
- 2 1/4 cups coconut milk
- 1 tablespoon palm sugar
- 1/2 teaspoon sea salt
- 5 kaffir lime leaves
- 1 red spur chili, sliced into rings
- cooked coconut cream and crisp-fried tofu for topping
- red spur chili slices and kaffir lime leaves for garnish
- Fresh vegetables: white turmeric, yard-long bean, Chinese cabbage, cucumber, assorted eggplants etc.

1. Bring a pot of water (with small amount of salt) over medium heat. Boil tofu until done and floated to the surface. Remove and cut into small pieces. Put aside.
2. In a mortar, pound dried chilies, galangal, lemongrass, kaffir lime rind, wild ginger and shallot finely. Add dark fermented soybean and pound to obtain a smooth paste. Add cooked tofu, pound well. Dip out into a bowl and put aside. This can make 1/4 cup of tofu mixture.
3. Cook coconut milk with tofu mixture prepared in step 2 over low heat until red oil surfaces and the thick sauce is obtained. Season well with palm sugar and salt. The taste should have a perfect balance of salty and sweet with an aromatic smell of wild ginger. Tear kaffir lime leaves before adding into the pan, add red spur chili and turn off the heat.
4. Dip out into a serving dish, top with cooked coconut cream and crisp-fried tofu. Garnish with red spur chili and kaffir lime leaves. It goes well with fresh vegetables.

(Serves 4)

This is the perfect dip that goes well with various kinds of fresh vegetables including white turmeric. This aromatic vegetable has its unique flavor and fragrance. Select those with white flesh and no bruise is seen. White turmeric can help to ease flatulent and relief gas.

Vegetarian Roasted Duck Curry

(kaeng phed ped yaang je)

- 1 cup vegetable oil
- 1/2 piece (125 grams) vegetarian roasted duck
- 3 cups coconut milk
- 1/2 cup Sriracha pineapple, cut into pieces
- 4 cherry tomatoes
- 1/2 tablespoon light soy sauce
- 1/2 tablespoon seasoning sauce
- 1/2 teaspoon sea salt
- 2 tablespoons palm sugar
- 1/2 kaffir lime, seeded
- 1/2 cup sweet basil leaves
- sweet basil leaves for garnish

Curry paste

- 5 cloves Thai garlic, peeled
- 3 shallots, sliced
- 1/2 cup red curry paste (page 18)

1. To make curry paste: Put garlic and shallots in a mortar and pound finely. Add red curry paste and pound to a fine mixture.
2. Place a pan with oil over medium heat. When the oil is hot, fry a whole piece of roasted duck until lightly golden. Remove and drain. Slice thinly and put aside.
3. In another pan, boil 1/2 cup of coconut milk over medium heat until boiling and oil surfaces. Sauté the curry paste until fragrant and the sauce reduce. Transfer to a pot and place over medium heat, add the remaining coconut milk, stir. Add pineapple and tomatoes. Season to taste with light soy sauce, seasoning sauce, salt and palm sugar. When it boils, put in kaffir lime and roasted duck, stir to combine. Scatter basil leaves over the top and turn off the heat.
4. Garnish with sweet basil leaves before serving.

(Serves 4)

Kaffir lime brings its unique aroma and zesty taste to the dish. The curry should have red oil over the surface and a perfect balance of salty, sweet and sour. The sweet and sour taste come from fruits such as pineapple, tomato, apple and plum mango. Tamarind juice may be added if preferred. It is recommended to fry vegetarian roasted duck before adding to the curry to obtain a firm texture and a tempting aroma.

Red Curry with Assorted Mushrooms

(kaeng phed hed)

- 1 cup coconut cream
- $^1/_2$ cup red curry paste (page 18)
- 15 straw mushrooms, cut
- 100 grams small angel mushrooms
- 100 grams oyster mushrooms, torn into pieces
- $3^1/_2$ cups coconut milk
- $^1/_2$ teaspoon sea salt
- 2 tablespoons light soy sauce
- $^1/_4$ cup wild ginger, shredded
- 1 each red and green spur chilies, cut diagonally
- $^1/_2$ cup sweet basil leaves
- sweet basil sprig for garnish

1. Cook coconut cream in a pan until oil surfaces, using medium heat. Add in red curry paste and cook until fragrant and red oil surfaces. Add all mushrooms and coconut milk. When everything is done, season to taste with salt and light soy sauce (add small amount of palm sugar if preferred). When it boils, add wild ginger, spur chilies and sweet basil leaves. When it boils again, turn off the heat.
2. Ladle into a serving bowl and garnish with sweet basil sprig before serving.

(Serves 4)

Shredded wild ginger adds unique flavor and fragrance to the curry. Select those with fresh plump roots, they will be juicy, hot and full of aroma. Wash well and lightly scrape off the skin. Wash again and shred or finely slice before adding to required dishes.

Green Curry with Long Green Eggplants

(kaeng khiaw waan)

- 2 (150 grams each) long green eggplants
- 8 large pieces textured vegetable protein (TVP)
- 1 cup coconut cream
- ½ cup green curry paste (page 19)
- 3 cups coconut milk
- 3 tablespoons light soy sauce
- 1 tablespoon palm sugar
- ½ cup sweet basil leaves
- 7 kaffir lime leaves, torn

1. Wash eggplants, cut into 1" sections and halve each lengthwise. Soak in a bowl of lightly salted water to prevent from discoloration.
2. In a pot of water, add a pinch of salt and place over medium heat. Bring to the boil, add TVP and cook until tender. Remove, soak in cold water for a few minutes and squeeze to dry. Cut into pieces and put aside.
3. Put coconut cream in another pan and place over medium heat. When the oil surfaces, add green curry paste. Sauté until fragrant and green oil appears on the surface. Add TVP, toss to coat well. Transfer to a curry pot, pour in coconut milk and stir to combine. Season to taste with light soy sauce and palm sugar. The sauce should taste spicy, salty and creamy sweet. When it boils, add eggplants and cook until done. Sprinkle on top with sweet basil leaves and kaffir lime leaves. Turn off the heat.
4. Enjoy while hot with steamed rice or fermented rice vermicelli.

(Serves 4)

Long green eggplant is tender and sweet when cooked. Select young fruits with a light green skin as those with dark green skin are mature, have plenty of seeds with flabby flesh.

Wax Gourd and Tofu Curry

(kaeng khua fuk kub tao-hoo)

- 1 piece (250 grams) hard white tofu
- 250 grams mature wax gourd
- 1 cup coconut cream
- 3 tablespoons *kaeng khua* curry paste
- 2 cups coconut milk
- 3 tablespoons light soy sauce
- 1/2 teaspoon sea salt
- 1 tablespoon+1 teaspoon palm sugar
- 2 tablespoons tamarind juice
- 3 kaffir lime leaves, torn
- 1 red spur chili, sliced diagonally

Kaeng khua curry paste

- 5 dried red spur chilies, seeded and soaked until tender
- 1/4 teaspoon sea salt
- 1 teaspoon mature galangal, finely sliced
- 1 tablespoon lemongrass, finely sliced
- 20 cloves Thai garlic, peeled
- 10 shallots, finely sliced
- 1 tablespoon dark fermented soybean

1. To prepare *kaeng khua* curry paste: In a mortar, pound dried chilies and salt finely. Add galangal, lemongrass, garlic and shallots and pound well. Add dark fermented soybean, continue pounding until a smooth paste is obtained. Put aside.
2. Bring a pot of water (with small amount of salt) over medium heat. Boil tofu until done and floated to the surface to obtain firm and chewy texture. Remove and leave to cool. Diagonally cut tofu into pieces and put aside.
3. Cut wax gourd into halves, discard seeds and peel. Wash and cut to obtain 1 inch pieces. Put aside.
4. Cook coconut cream in a pan over medium heat until oil surfaces. Fry curry paste until fragrant and red oil surfaces. Add in boiled tofu and toss well. Transfer to a curry pot and add coconut milk. Stir well and cook until boiling. Add wax gourd, continue boiling until the wax gourd is cooked through. Season to taste with light soy sauce, salt, sugar and tamarind juice. When it boils again, add kaffir lime leaves and red spur chili, remove from the heat.
5. Dip out into a serving dish and serve.

(Serves 4)

This dish has a perfect combination of sweet, rich and medium hot tastes. The red oil over its surface makes it look tempting. Mature wax gourd is used in this recipe for its sweet and tender flesh. Buy the gourd of about 1 kilogram in weight, its thick flesh will not become too soft when cooked.

Sour Soup with Mixed Vegetables

(kaeng som phak ruam)

- $3^1/_2$ cups water or vegetarian noodle stock (version 2 page 15)
- $^1/_4$ cup sour curry paste (page 19)
- $^1/_4$ cup+2 tablespoons tamarind juice
- 1 teaspoon palm sugar
- $1^1/_2$ tablespoons light soy sauce
- 1 teaspoon sea salt
- 100 grams straw mushrooms, quartered
- 1 (200 grams) Chinese radish, sliced crosswise
- 150 grams green papaya, sliced
- 4 pods yard-long bean, cut into 1" sections
- 100 grams Chinese cabbage, cut into bite-sized pieces
- 50 grams fried dried bean curd skin

1. Place a pot of water or stock over medium heat and bring to the boil. Stir in curry paste, season well with tamarind juice, palm sugar, light soy sauce and salt. The taste should be sour, salty and sweet. Add mushrooms and cook until done. Add Chinese radish and green papaya, continue cooking until done. Then add in yard-long bean, Chinese cabbage and fried bean curd skin. Boil for a few minutes, remove from the heat.
2. Transfer to a serving dish and serve hot.

(Serves 4)

There are 3 types of sun-dried tamarind sold in the market: seeded tamarind with its fibrous net, tamarind with seed but no fibrous net and pure tamarind flesh. The first and the last types are both popularly used.

Jungle Curry

(kaeng paa)

- 4 cups water or vegetable stock (version 1 page 13)
- 1/3-1/2 cup jungle curry paste (page 21)
- 1 piece (200 grams) hard white tofu, boiled and cut into pieces
- 250 grams pumpkin, cut into pieces
- 3 Thai eggplants, quartered
- 1/2 cup pea eggplants
- 1/4 cup light soy sauce
- 1 teaspoon sea salt
- 1/2 teaspoon unbleached sugar
- 1/2 cup holy basil leaves
- shredded wild ginger for garnish

1. In a pot of water or stock, add jungle curry paste and stir to dissolve well. Bring to a boil over medium heat. Add tofu, pumpkin and both kinds of eggplants. When everything is cooked through, season to taste with light soy sauce, salt and sugar. It should have a balanced taste of salty and spicy. When it boils again, add holy basil leaves, stir lightly and remove from the heat.
2. Dip out into a serving bowl and garnish with wild ginger before serving.

(Serves 4-6)

Holy basil, a hot and aromatic Thai herb, is available both wild and commercially-grown types. Wild holy basil has small leaves, strong aroma and is peppery hot while commercially-grown holy basil has larger leaves with milder aroma. Add holy basil only when the soup is boiling to obtain its strong fragrance.

Southern Yellow Curry

(kaeng leung sa-tor kub nor-mai-dong)

- 7 dried shiitake mushrooms
- 2 cups vegetable oil
- 2 pods stinky bean
- 300 grams pickled bamboo shoot
- 3 cups water
- 5 pieces garcenia
- 9 straw mushrooms, quartered
- 1 teaspoon sea salt
- 1 tablespoon light soy sauce
- 1 tablespoon seasoning sauce
- 3 tablespoons tamarind juice
- 2 tablespoons palm sugar
- 10 pieces dried bean curd skin, tied and soaked until tender
- 1 tablespoon lime juice

Curry paste

- 2 shallots, sliced
- 1/4 cup Southern yellow curry paste (page 20)
- 2 tablespoons dark fermented soybean

1. To make curry paste: Pound shallots and yellow curry paste together well. Add fermented soybean and pound to obtain a fine paste, put aside.
2. Wash shiitake mushrooms, soak in a bowl of water until tender, squeeze and cut away hard stems. Fry in hot oil until golden and fragrant, put aside.
3. Wash stinky bean, cut into sections, cut away the edges and lightly scrape off green pod. Wash again and drain.
4. Wash pickled bamboo shoot and put into a pot. Pour water to cover and boil over medium heat for 10-15 minutes (to reduce the sourness). Turn off the heat. Wash again and drain.
5. Stir the curry paste in a pot of water and place over medium heat. When it boils, add bamboo shoot, stinky bean and garcenia. Cook for a moment or until the soup tastes sour, add both mushrooms. Season with salt, light soy sauce, seasoning sauce, tamarind juice and palm sugar. Stir to mix well, add bean curd skin. When everything is done, remove from the heat. Stir in lime juice, taste and adjust to your liking. The curry should tastes sour, salty and spicy.
6. Best when serve with steamed rice.

(Serves 3-4)

Mushrooms and bean curd skin provide protein to this dish. Select young straw mushroom with firm and tasty texture. For dried shiitake mushroom, it should be soaked in water until tender, squeezed and trimmed away hard stem before frying until lightly golden to obtain an aromatic and chewy texture.

Vegetarian Fish's Entrails Curry

(kaeng tai-plaa je)

- 1 sheet (20 grams) soup seaweed
- 1/4 cup light soy sauce
- 7 straw mushrooms
- 50 grams angel mushrooms
- 50 grams abalone mushrooms
- 8 cups water
- 2 teaspoons palm sugar
- 100 grams fresh bamboo shoot, cut into pieces
- 100 grams pumpkin, cut into pieces
- 300 grams boiled jackfruit seeds
- 3 Thai eggplants, quartered
- 8 stinky beans, peeled
- 4 pods yard-long bean, cut into 1" pieces
- 50 grams pea eggplant
- 5 pods winged bean, cut into 1" pieces
- 7 kaffir lime leaves
- 2 tablespoons green peppercorns
- 2 kilograms fermented rice vermicelli
- green peppercorn sprigs for garnish
- Fresh vegetables: winged bean, stinky bean, bean sprouts, cashew nut tips, yard-long bean, etc.

Curry paste

- 100 grams vegetarian fish's entrails curry paste (page 21)
- 1/4 cup+1 tablespoon dark fermented soybean
- 7 cubes red fermented tofu, fried until lightly golden

1. Grill the seaweed over low heat until fragrant (Do not use high heat as it will be burnt easily). Tear into pieces and marinate in light soy sauce for at least 1 day in a room temperature. The longer time you use for marinating, the better taste it will obtain.
2. To make curry paste: Pound fish's entrails curry paste, fermented soybean and fried fermented tofu together to a fine paste. Put aside.
3. Grill all the mushrooms over medium heat until fragrant and done. Tear into pieces and pound together well. Put aside.
4. Bring a pot of water to the boil. Add curry paste and palm sugar, stir to dissolve. Put in bamboo shoot, pounded mushrooms, pumpkin, boiled jackfruit seeds and marinated seaweed. Cook until boiling and the pumpkin is done. Add Thai eggplants and stinky beans, cook until done. Add yard-long bean, cracked pea eggplant and winged bean. Tear kaffir lime leaves into pieces and put in. Add green peppercorns, remove from the heat.
5. Dip out into a serving dish and garnish with green peppercorn sprigs. This curry goes well with fermented rice vermicelli and fresh vegetables.

(Serves 8-10)

The vegetarian fish's entrails are made from marinating seaweed in light soy sauce for many months. Glutamic acid in the seaweed makes this dish tastes as good as the one cooked with meat added. A salty taste comes from dark fermented soybean and fried red fermented tofu.

Mussamun Curry

(kaeng mus-sa-mun)

100 grams large-sized textured vegetable protein (TVP)
1 cup coconut cream
2 cups coconut milk
½ potato, cut into 1.5 cm. cubes
½ tablespoon seasoning sauce
1 tablespoon light soy sauce
¼ cup+2 tablespoons tamarind juice
3 tablespoons palm sugar
1 teaspoon sea salt
2 bay leaves
1 cup Phuket pineapple, cut into 1.5 cm. cubes
1 onion, cut into 1.5 cm cubes
½ cup+2 tablespoons roasted peanut
bay leaves and diagonally-cut red spur chilies for garnish

Curry paste

2 pods cardamom
½ nutmeg
2 teaspoons coriander seeds
1 teaspoon cumin
3 shallots, sliced
15 cloves Thai garlic, peeled
½ cup+1 tablespoon mussamun curry paste (page 20)

1. To make curry paste: Dry-fry or roast cardamom, nutmeg, coriander seeds and cumin in a pan over low heat until fragrant. Remove from the heat. Transfer to a mortar and pound to a fine powder. Add shallots and garlic, pound well. Add mussamun curry paste, continue pounding until a smooth paste is obtained.
2. Place a pot of water over medium heat and bring to the boil. Boil TVP until tender, remove and transfer to soak in cold water for a few minutes. Squeeze to dry, cut into pieces and set aside.
3. Boil ½ cup of coconut cream over medium heat until boiling and oil surfaces. Sauté curry paste until fragrant and red oil surfaces. Add 1 cup of coconut milk and stir. Transfer to a pot and bring back to medium heat. Boil until red oil surfaces, add cooked TVP and potato. Season to taste with seasoning sauce, light soy sauce, tamarind juice, palm sugar and salt. The curry should have a taste of sour, salty and sweet. Add in bay leaves, pineapple and onion. Pour in the remaining coconut liquid and continue cooking until everything is done. Stir in roasted peanut and turn off the heat.
4. Dip out into a serving dish, garnish with bay leaves and spur chilies before serving.

(Serves 6-8)

The curry sauce is quite thick and has plenty of red oil over the surface. Phuket pineapple is used in this recipe as it has a sweet and sour taste and a crisp flesh. Roasted peanut is added only when the curry sauce thickens as to maintain its crispiness.

Panaeng Curry

(pa-naeng)

- 70 grams large-sized textured vegetable protein (TVP)
- 3 1/2 cups coconut milk
- 5 straw mushrooms, quartered
- 1 abalone mushroom, sliced thinly
- 1/2 teaspoon sea salt
- 1 tablespoon+2 teaspoons palm sugar
- 1 tablespoon light soy sauce
- 1 tablespoon seasoning sauce
- 1/2 cup pea eggplant, lightly cracked
- 2 kaffir lime leaves
- 1/2 cup sweet basil leaves
- 2 green and red spur chilies, sliced diagonally
- shredded and whole kaffir lime leaves for garnish

Curry paste

- 2 pods cardamom
- 5 cloves
- 2 teaspoons coriander seeds
- 1 teaspoon cumin
- 1/2 nutmeg
- 2 coriander roots, sliced
- 3 shallots, sliced
- 15 cloves Thai garlic, peeled
- 1/2 cup red curry paste (page 18)

1. To make curry paste: Dry-fry or roast cardamom, cloves, coriander seeds, cumin and nutmeg over low heat until fragrant. Remove from the heat. In a mortar, pound coriander roots finely. Add roasted spices and pound well. Add shallots and garlic, pound thoroughly before adding red curry paste. Continue pounding until a smooth curry mixture is obtained.
2. Bring a pot of water to the boil over medium heat. Cook TVP until tender, remove and soak in cold water. Squeeze to dry and cut into thin slices.
3. Boil 1/2 cup of coconut milk in a pot until it boils and oil surfaces. Add curry mixture and sauté until fragrant and red oil surfaces. Add cooked TVP, stir to combine. Add another cup of coconut milk. Cook until boils well and red oil surfaces. Add both mushrooms, cook until done. Pour in the remaining coconut milk. Season to taste with salt, palm sugar, light soy sauce and seasoning sauce. Add pea eggplant and torn kaffir lime leaves. When it boils again, add sweet basil leaves and spur chilies, stir lightly. Remove from the heat.
4. Dip out into a serving dish, sprinkle shredded and whole kaffir lime leaves over the top and serve.

(Serves 4-6)

Large-sized textured vegetable protein is used in this recipe. Dark TVP is used to substitute beef while plain TVP is a good replacement for chicken and pork. It should be boiled until tender to reduce its nutty or oily smell. Cut TVP into large thin slices to enable it to absorb the sauce well.

Tofu in Chu Chee Sauce

(chu-chee tao-hoo)

- 2 pieces (230 grams each) yellow tofu
- 2 cups vegetable oil
- 1 cup coconut cream
- 1/2 cup *chu chee* curry paste
- 1 cup coconut milk
- 1 tablespoon light soy sauce
- 2 teaspoons palm sugar
- 1/4 teaspoon sea salt
- 2 tablespoons kaffir lime leaves, shredded
- 1 red spur chili, shredded
- cooked coconut cream for topping
- diagonally cut red spur chili and fried kaffir lime leaves for garnish

***Chu chee* curry paste** (1/2 cup)

- 7 dried red spur chilies, seeded and soaked until tender
- 1/2 teaspoon sea salt
- 2 teaspoons mature galangal, finely sliced
- 2 tablespoons lemongrass, sliced
- 1 teaspoon kaffir lime rind, finely sliced
- 1 teaspoon coriander root, sliced
- 1/4 cup Thai garlic, peeled
- 7 shallots, sliced
- 1 tablespoon dark fermented soybean

1. To prepare *chu chee* curry paste: Pound dried chilies and salt together well. Add galangal, lemongrass, kaffir lime rind, coriander root and garlic, pound finely. Add shallots and dark fermented soybean and continue pounding until a smooth paste is obtained. Put aside.
2. Bring a pot of water (with small amount of salt) over medium heat. Put in yellow tofu and boil until done and floated to the surface. Remove and drain (its texture will become firm and chewy). Cut diagonally to obtain large pieces. Fry tofu in hot oil over medium heat until golden on all sides. Remove from the pan and drain.
3. Heat coconut cream in a pan over medium heat until oil surfaces. Fry curry paste until fragrant, add fried tofu and coconut milk. Cook until the sauce thickens. Season with light soy sauce, palm sugar and salt. Add shredded kaffir lime leaves and red spur chili, turn off the heat.
4. Transfer to a serving dish, top with cooked coconut cream and garnish attractively with red spur chili and fried kaffir lime leaves.

(Serves 4)

Yellow tofu is a bit saltier than white tofu as it is marinated in salted water before being boiled in a solution of water and turmeric. The curry paste used to make *chu chee* sauce is "*kaeng khua*" curry paste which has the same ingredients as the red curry paste but omit the spices. The finished curry sauce should be reddish orange with a sweet flavor.

Spicy Stir-Fried TVP

(phad phrik khing)

- 3 cups vegetable oil
- 70 grams textured vegetable protein (TVP)
- 2 tablespoons water
- 2½ tablespoons palm sugar
- 1 tablespoon light soy sauce
- 1 teaspoon sea salt
- 3 tablespoons roasted sesame seeds
- 2 tablespoons shredded kaffir lime leaves
- 1 red spur chili, shredded
- green ork leaves for garnish

Chili paste

- 7 dried red spur chilies, seeded and soaked until tender
- ½ teaspoon sea salt
- 2 stems lemongrass, thinly sliced
- ½ teaspoon kaffir lime rind, finely sliced
- 35 cloves Thai garlic, peeled
- 1 teaspoon mature galangal, finely sliced
- 2 teaspoons roasted coriander seeds
- 3 coriander roots, sliced
- 6 shallots, sliced
- 3 tablespoons ground salted mushroom
- 2 teaspoons vegetarian shrimp paste or dark fermented soybean

Ground salted mushroom

- 250 grams angel mushroom
- ¼ teaspoon sea salt

1. To prepare salted mushroom: Clean angel mushroom with cloth, cut away hard stems and squeeze to dry. Slice or coarsely chop, toss well with salt. Leave for 5-10 minutes and squeeze to dry. Place a pan over low heat and dry-fry the mushroom until completely dry. Transfer to a mortar and pound until fluffy.
2. To prepare chili paste: Pound dried chilies and salt thoroughly. Add lemongrass, kaffir lime rind, garlic, galangal, coriander seeds and roots, and shallots. Pound to a fine paste. Add salted mushroom, vegetarian shrimp paste or dark fermented soybean and pound to mix well. (Salted mushroom is added to help fried TVP coat well with the chili paste.)
3. Place a pan of oil over medium heat and wait until the oil is hot. Fry TVP until golden crispy. Remove and drain.
4. Drain off the oil in the pan and leave only 3 tablespoons, mix chili paste with water and put in, sauté until fragrant. Season to taste with palm sugar, light soy sauce and salt. Stir well. Add fried TVP and toss to coat well. Scatter sesame seeds over and toss to combine. Remove from the heat.
5. Line green ork leaves on a serving dish and spoon spicy stir-fried TVP over. Sprinkle shredded kaffir lime leaves and red spur chili on top. Serve hot with steamed rice.

(Serves 4)

Plain textured vegetable protein is a good substitution for pork. Use the flat or small ones for this recipe. Fry them in batch to maintain the oil temperature and to obtain a nice golden color.

Stir-Fried Long Green Eggplant

(phad ma-kheu-yao)

- 3 tablespoons vegetable oil
- 1 tablespoon garlic, chopped
- 100 grams hard white tofu, mashed and fried until just golden
- 1 long green eggplant (220-250 grams), cut diagonally and soaked in light salted water
- 1/4 cup vegetable stock (version 1 page 13)
- 1 tablespoon dark fermented soybean
- 1 teaspoons light soy sauce
- 1 1/2 teaspoons sugar
- 1 red spur chili, cut into strips
- 1/2 cup sweet basil leaves
- sweet basil sprig for garnish

1. Preheat a pan of oil over medium heat. When the oil is hot, fry chopped garlic until golden and fragrant. Add fried tofu and green eggplant, toss to combine. Add stock and cook until the eggplant is done. Season to taste with fermented soybean, light soy sauce and sugar. Cook for a few minutes, add spur chili strips and sweet basil leaves. Toss well and turn off the heat.
2. Ladle into a serving dish and garnish with sweet basil sprig.

(Serves 2)

Hard white tofu is mashed to resemble minced pork and to help absorb the seasoning. It is fried before adding to the dish in order to maintain its texture and gain more aromas.

Crisp-Fried Tofu in Red Curry Sauce

(phad phed plaa-duk je thod krob)

- 2 pieces (200 grams each) hard white tofu
- 3 tablespoons light soy sauce
- 3 sheets nori seaweed (about 7" wide and 8" long)
- 3 cups vegetable oil
- 1 egg, beaten
- $^1/_4$-$^1/_3$ cup red curry paste (page 18)
- 2 teaspoons palm sugar
- $^1/_4$ cup green peppercorns, cut into sections
- $^1/_4$ cup wild ginger, shredded
- 8 crisp-fried kaffir lime leaves
- $^1/_4$ cup crisp-fried holy basil leaves
- 1 red spur chili, shredded

A large sheet of nori seaweed, normally used for sushi roll, is recommended for this recipe. Take the seaweed out of the pack only when used. Work on the dry surface as it will be easily torn when wet. Brush the edge with water or egg white to seal, steam until heated through and leave to cool in a refrigerator. Cut to obtain thick slices, dip in lightly beaten egg and deep-fry until golden crispy.

1. Bring a pot of water to the boil over high heat (add small amount of salt before boiling). Put in tofu and boil until done and floated to the surface. Remove, transfer to a mixing bowl and allow to cool. Mash boiled tofu and toss with 2 tablespoons of light soy sauce. Put aside.
2. Place nori seaweed on a flat surface. Spoon mashed tofu along one side of the seaweed sheet. Wrap and roll into 1" in diameter, brush the edge with water and seal tightly. Continue until finished. Steam over hot boiling water for 5 minutes, using medium heat. When done, remove and allow to cool in a refrigerator before cutting into slices about 1" thick.
3. Place a pan of oil over medium-low heat. When the oil is slightly hot, dip the tofu slices in beaten egg and fry until golden crispy (fry 6 slices at a time). Remove and drain.
4. Drain off the oil and leave only $^1/_4$ cup in the pan. Sauté curry paste in hot oil until fragrant. Season with the remaining light soy sauce and palm sugar. Add green peppercorns and wild ginger. Stir-fry to mix well, add fried tofu and toss to combine. Turn off the heat.
5. Arrange on a serving plate, garnish with crisp-fried kaffir lime leaves, holy basil leaves and red spur chili. Serve at once.

(Serves 4)

Stir-Fried Mixed Vegetables

(phad phak ruam-mid)

- 3 tablespoons vegetable oil
- 1 tablespoon garlic, chopped
- 1 (250 grams) carrot, sliced
- 1 (250 grams) broccoli, cut into pieces
- 10 ears baby corn, cut into 2" sections
- 10 fresh small shiitake mushrooms, trimmed away hard stalks
- 10 straw mushrooms, quartered
- 1/4 teaspoon sea salt
- 1 tablespoon light soy sauce
- 3 tablespoons vegetarian oyster sauce
- 2 teaspoons sugar
- fried garlic for topping
- diagonally sliced red spur chili for garnish

1. Preheat the oil in a pan over medium heat. When the oil is hot, fry chopped garlic until fragrant and golden. Add in carrot, broccoli, baby corn, shiitake mushrooms and straw mushrooms. Add salt and stir-fry until everything is done. Season well with light soy sauce, vegetarian oyster sauce and sugar. Toss to mix well and remove from the heat.
2. Ladle into a serving dish, sprinkle fried garlic and sliced spur chili over the top. Serve hot.

(Serves 4)

Vegetarian oyster sauce is made from shiitake mushrooms, soy sauce, sugar, salt and glucose syrup. The slightly thick sauce has a light brown color with salty and sweet tastes. It is good to add in many stir-fried dishes. Look for manufacturing date on its label when purchasing.

Stir-Fried Eryngii Mushrooms with Holy Basil

(phad ka-phrao hed eryngii)

- 250 grams eryngii mushrooms
- 31 hot chilies
- 5 large red hot chilies
- 25 cloves small Thai garlic
- 3 coriander roots, sliced
- 1/4 teaspoon sea salt
- 3 tablespoons vegetable oil
- 1/4 cup vegetable stock (version 1 page 13)
- 2 tablespoons light soy sauce
- 1/2 teaspoon sugar
- 1 cup holy basil leaves
- crisp-fried holy basil leaves for garnish

1. Clean eryngii mushrooms with a towel, cut into small cubes and put aside.
2. Coarsely pound hot chilies, large hot chilies, garlic, coriander roots and salt. Put aside.
3. Preheat a pan with oil over medium heat. When the oil is hot, sauté chili mixture until fragrant. Add mushrooms and stock and cook until done. Season to taste with light soy sauce and sugar. Toss to combine. Add holy basil leaves and continue cooking until fragrant. Turn off the heat.
4. Dip out into a serving dish and garnish with crisp-fried holy basil leaves before serving.

(Serves 2-3)

Eryngii mushroom which has a white plump stem and a small cap is known as a good replacement for meat. Its thick flesh is suit for grilling, stir-frying, and adding to curries. Quickly cook it in order to maintain its chewy texture.

White Tofu in Mild Curry Sauce

(tao-hoo phad phong ka-ree)

- 1 piece semi-hard white tofu (150 grams)
- 2 cups vegetable oil
- 1 tablespoon vegetarian roasted chili paste
- 1 teaspoon curry powder
- $\frac{1}{2}$ teaspoon sea salt
- $1\frac{1}{2}$ tablespoons unbleached sugar
- 1 tablespoon light soy sauce
- $\frac{1}{4}$ cup fresh milk
- 1 egg
- 1 teaspoon chopped garlic
- 25 grams onion
- 3 straw mushrooms, sliced
- 50 grams small angel mushrooms
- 1 spring onion, cut into $1\frac{1}{2}$" segments
- 1 Chinese celery, cut into 2" segments
- 1 red spur chili, cut diagonally
- Chinese celery sprig for garnish

Vegetarian roasted chili paste ($\frac{1}{4}$ cup)

- 7 dried red spur chilies, sliced and roasted
- 4 shallots, sliced
- 2 tablespoons Thai garlic, peeled and roasted
- 3 tablespoons olive oil

Curry powder is widely used in making curry. It consists of several spices such as coriander seed, cumin, turmeric, fenugreek and so on. The curry powder is available both in bottle and packet forms. Always keep in a cool dry place.

1. To prepare vegetarian roasted chili paste: Pound everything to a fine paste with a mortar and a pestle. Sauté 1 tablespoon of the chili paste with olive oil over low heat until fragrant to obtain roasted chili paste oil. Turn off the heat and put aside.
2. Bring a pot of water (with a dash of salt) to the boil over medium heat. Add in tofu and cook until it floats to the surface. Remove to soak in a bowl of water until cold. Drain and pat-dry, cut cooked tofu into quarters and put aside.
3. Place a pan over medium heat and put in oil. When the oil is very hot, fry cooked tofu until golden on all sides. Remove and drain.
4. In a mixing bowl, combine the remaining chili paste with $1\frac{1}{2}$ tablespoons of roasted chili paste oil prepared in step 1. Add curry powder, salt, sugar, light soy sauce, milk and egg. Stir lightly just to break the egg, put aside.
5. Drain away the oil in the frying pan and leave only 3 tablespoons in the pan. Place the pan over medium heat and leave until it is hot. Fry chopped garlic until fragrant. Add onion, straw mushrooms, angel mushrooms and fried tofu. Toss to combine. Add in the egg mixture and leave until it begins to set. Stir and toss lightly. Add spring onion, Chinese celery and red spur chili. Continue to cook until the egg mixture is done. Turn off the heat.
6. Ladle into a serving dish and garnish with Chinese celery sprig. Serve hot.

(Serves 2-3)

Stir-Fried Mung Bean Noodles with Mixed Vegetables

(phad wun-sen)

- 1 pack (100 grams) dried mung bean noodles
- 1/4 cup vegetable oil
- 1 tablespoon garlic, chopped
- 250 grams cabbage, cut into pieces
- 50 grams dried lily flowers, soaked and tied to a knot
- 100 grams fresh black ear mushrooms, cut
- 1 cup vegetable stock (version 1 page 13)
- 2 tablespoons vegetarian oyster sauce
- 2 teaspoons seasoning sauce
- 2 teaspoons light soy sauce
- 1 teaspoon sugar
- 1 teaspoon pepper
- 1 teaspoon Chinese rice wine
- 1/2 cup crisp-fried dried bean curd skin
- Chinese celery for garnish

1. Soak mung bean noodles in water for 12 minutes or until tender, drain and cut into short sections.
2. Preheat a pan of oil over medium heat. Fry chopped garlic until fragrant and golden. Add cabbage, dried lily flowers and black ear mushrooms. Stir-fry to combine. Add mung bean noodles and stock, toss again. Season well with vegetarian oyster sauce, seasoning sauce, light soy sauce, sugar, pepper and Chinese rice wine. Toss and stir-fry to mix well, turn off the heat.
3. Dip out into a serving dish and top with crisp-fried dried bean curd skin. Garnish with Chinese celery before serving.

(Serves 4)

Dried bean curd skin can be added to soup with mung bean noodles, deep-fried and served with sweet chili sauce as a snack or served as a condiment to fried rice. In this recipe, it is added to give crunchiness to the dish. The tofu sheet has already been cooked; just fry it in hot oil over low heat until fluffy and crispy before adding to the dish.

Pan-Fried Shiitake Mushrooms

(hed khua khem)

- 30 fresh medium-sized shiitake mushrooms
- 3 cups vegetable oil
- 1 tablespoon light soy sauce
- 1 teaspoon seasoning sauce
- 1/2 teaspoon brown sugar
- 1/2 teaspoon ground black pepper
- green ork leaves and carrot slices for garnish

1. Clean shiitake mushrooms with cloth or kitchen towel. Fry in hot oil over moderate heat until golden. Remove and put aside. Drain off the oil and leave only 1 tablespoon in the pan. Reduce the heat to low, return fried shiitake mushrooms to the pan. Season with light soy sauce, seasoning sauce, sugar and pepper and toss to coat well. Turn off the heat.
2. Arrange on a serving dish, garnish with green ork leaves and carrot slices.

(Serves 4)

Fresh shiitake mushroom will be more aromatic when being fried. Its texture will be firm and chewy with a stronger flavor. Do not wash the mushrooms; just softly wipe them with cloth or kitchen towel to remove dirt. Fry in hot oil over medium heat until they are golden. Do not fry until no bubble remains in the pan as the mushrooms will be over-fried and have a bitter taste.

Stir-Fried Stinky Bean in Curry Sauce

(phad sa-tor kreung-kaeng)

- 2 tablespoons vegetable oil
- 7 straw mushrooms, quartered
- 50 grams abalone mushrooms, torn
- 50 grams angel mushrooms, torn
- 1/4 cup water
- 1 tablespoon seasoning sauce
- 1 tablespoon light soy sauce
- 1 tablespoon palm sugar
- 150 grams stinky bean
- 1/2 cup sweet basil leaves
- 3 kaffir lime leaves, torn
- 2 sprigs green peppercorn, cut into sections
- 1 green spur chili, diagonally sliced
- 1 red spur chili, diagonally sliced
- kaffir lime leaves and green peppercorn sprigs for garnish

Curry paste

- 11 cloves Thai garlic, peeled
- 2 shallots, sliced
- 1/4 cup Southern red curry paste (page 18)
- 1 teaspoon vegetarian shrimp paste or dark fermented soybean

1. To make curry paste: In a mortar, thoroughly pound garlic, shallots and Southern red curry paste. Add vegetarian shrimp paste or dark fermented soybean and pound well. Put aside.
2. Place a pan over medium heat and put in oil. When the oil is hot, sauté curry paste until fragrant. Add all mushrooms, and stir-fry quickly until done. Add water and season to taste with seasoning sauce, light soy sauce and palm sugar. Toss to mix well. Add stinky bean and toss again. Add sweet basil leaves, kaffir lime leaves, green peppercorn and spur chilies stir to combine. Turn off the heat.
3. Dip out in a serving bowl, garnish with kaffir lime leaves and green peppercorn sprigs before serving.

(Serves 3-4)

Abalone mushrooms have thick and tender texture. Use a piece of cloth to clean them before cooking. Trim off the base, slightly bruise the stalks with a knife and cut into pieces as required, this will enable them to absorb the sauce well.

Spicy Stir-Fried Enoki Mushrooms

(hed-khem-thong phad chaa)

200 grams enoki mushrooms
3 tablespoons vegetable oil
1/4 cup spicy chili mixture
1/2 cup vegetable stock (version 1 page 13)
2 tablespoons light soy sauce
½ teaspoon palm sugar
2 tablespoons green peppercorn, cracked
green peppercorn sprig, red hot chili and kaffir lime leaves for garnish

Spicy chili mixture

11 dried hot chilies
2 large red hot chilies
1 teaspoon black pepper
2 teaspoons mature galangal, finely sliced
1 tablespoon coriander root, sliced
1 teaspoon kaffir lime rind, finely sliced
3 tablespoons small Thai garlic

1. To prepare spicy chili mixture: Pound dried hot chilies and large hot chilies together well. Add pepper, galangal, coriander root, kaffir lime rind and garlic. Pound to obtain a smooth paste.
2. Cut away the hard part of enoki mushrooms about 2 cm. from the base. Clean with a piece of cloth and put aside.
3. Place a pan of oil over high heat until the oil is hot. Sauté chili mixture until fragrant. Add in stock and enoki mushrooms. Stir-fry quickly until done. Season to taste with light soy sauce and sugar. Add green peppercorn, stir to mix well and remove from the heat.
4. Dip out into a serving dish and garnish with green peppercorn sprig, hot chili and kaffir lime leaves before serving.

(Serves 4)

Enoki mushroom requires a very short cooking time as it tends to be tough easily. Buy only the quantity you need and keep the remaining unwashed and refrigerated in a tightly-sealed bag.

Stir-Fried Chayote

(yod ma-ra-waan fai daeng)

100 grams chayote, cut into sections about 5-6" from the tip
3 tablespoonsvegetable oil
6 cloves Thai garlic, peeled and crushed
10 red and green hot chilies, bruised
1 1/2 tablespoons light soy sauce
1 1/2 tablespoons vegetarian oyster sauce
1 teaspoon sugar
1/4 cup water or vegetable stock (version 3 page 14)
1 teaspoon fried garlic

1. Wash chayote well and drain.
2. Place a wok of oil over high heat until the oil is very hot. Add garlic and hot chilies, stir quickly. Add in chayote, season with light soy sauce, oyster sauce, sugar and add some water or stock. Stir-fry quickly and remove from the heat.
3. Transfer to a serving dish, sprinkle fried garlic over the top and serve hot.

(Serves 2)

Chayote has sweet and crisp tips and is available all year round. But the perfect time is during the rainy season when the vegetable has the perfect appearance and very tasty. It contains calcium, phosphorous and a lot of beta-carotene.

Stir-Fried Preserved Chinese Radish with Egg

(phad hua-chai-po sai khai)

3 tablespoons vegetable oil
1 egg
1 1/2 cups sweet preserved Chinese radish, shredded
2 tablespoons chopped shallot
1/2 teaspoon sugar

1. Pre-heat a pan with oil over medium heat until the oil is hot. Break in an egg and stir. Put preserved Chinese radish over the egg and reduce to low heat. Cook until it sets then move to the side of the pan. Add in chopped shallot and sauté until fragrant. Toss the preserved radish with shallot and season with sugar. Stir-fry to combine, turn off the heat.
2. Dip out into a serving dish and serve.
(Serves 2)

Shredded sweet preserved Chinese radish is used in this recipe. Select those with a light brown color, are shiny and packed in a proper packaging. It is not necessary to wash them before using. The shallot added to this dish will provide a better aroma than the garlic.

Stir-Fried Vegetarian Chicken with Cashew Nuts

(kai je phad med-ma-muang-him-ma-phaan)

- 2 pieces (130 grams each) vegetarian chicken breast
- 3 cups vegetable oil
- 1/2 onion, diced
- 50 grams each red, green and yellow bell peppers, diced
- 1/2 cup fried cashew nuts
- 3 stems spring onion, cut into 1" sections
- 1 tablespoon+1 teaspoon sugar
- 3 tablespoons vegetarian oyster sauce
- 1 tablespoon seasoning sauce
- 2 tablespoons light soy sauce
- crisp-fried dried spur chilies, sliced for garnish

1. Diagonally slice vegetarian chicken breast into pieces, put aside.
2. Pre-heat a pan with oil over medium heat until the oil is hot, fry vegetarian chicken breast until golden and cooked through. Drain on absorbent paper.
3. Drain off the oil in the frying pan and leave only 3 tablespoons. Add onion, bell peppers, chicken breast, cashew nuts and spring onion. Fry quickly over high heat. Season to taste with sugar, oyster sauce, seasoning sauce and light soy sauce. Stir to mix well and turn off the heat.
4. Transfer to a serving dish and garnish with crisp-fried dried chilies. Enjoy while hot.

(Serves 2)

Vegetarian chicken breast is made from fresh bean curd skin, seasoned and pressed to resemble a real chicken breast. It is available both chilled and frozen types. The product will be a bit darker when kept frozen, but will return to its original color and taste after being thawed.

Stir-Fried Kale with Vegetarian Salted Fish

(phad kha-naa plaa khem je)

- 3 large kales
- 3 tablespoons vegetable oil
- 1 teaspoon garlic, coarsely chopped
- 1 tablespoon vegetarian oyster sauce
- 1/2 teaspoon unbleached sugar
- 1/2 teaspoon sweet dark soy sauce
- 1/4 cup water or vegetable stock (version 1 page 13)
- 7 hot chilies, crushed

Vegetarian salted fish

- 1 piece tube tofu (220 grams)
- 2 tablespoons light soy sauce
- 2 tablespoons seasoning sauce

1. To prepare vegetarian salted fish: Store tube tofu in a freezer until completely frozen (it is recommended to store it overnight). Bring the frozen tofu out off the freezer and thaw. Squeeze to dry and reserve only the solid part. Put into a mixing bowl and toss well with light soy sauce and seasoning sauce, leave to marinate.
2. Wash the kales, peel off tough outer skin and cut the stems diagonally to obtain ½" slices. Cut the leaves into 1" pieces. Blanch stems and leaves in hot boiling water and put aside.
3. Preheat a pan of oil over medium heat until the oil is hot. Fry chopped garlic until golden and fragrant. Add vegetarian salted fish, stir-fry until it smells fragrant and becomes golden. Season to taste with vegetarian oyster sauce, sugar, sweet dark soy sauce, toss to combine. Add kale and water or stock. Cook until everything is done, add hot chilies. Toss lightly and turn off the heat.
4. Dip out into a serving dish and serve.

(Serves 2)

Blanch the kale before stir-frying in order to make the vegetable looks brightly green when finished. Dark soy sauce is added to give a nice color to the dish. There are 2 types of dark soy sauce available: salty type and sweet type. Look for sweet dark soy sauce made from sugar; it has a better quality than the one made from molasses.

Tasty Shredded Mushroom

(hed yong)

- 300 grams angel mushrooms, shredded and squeezed to dry
- 2 teaspoons ground coriander seeds
- 1 teaspoon ground cumin
- 1 teaspoon sea salt
- $1\frac{1}{2}$ tablespoons seasoning sauce
- 1 tablespoon palm sugar
- 3 cups vegetable oil
- 2 tablespoons roasted white sesame seeds
- lettuce leaves and diagonally sliced carrot for garnish

1. In a mixing bowl, toss angel mushrooms with coriander seeds, cumin, salt, seasoning sauce and palm sugar. Spread on a tray and roast in an oven at 150 °C for 10-15 minutes or until just dry. Leave to cool. (The mushrooms can be sun-dried instead of being roast).
2. Place a frying pan with oil over moderate heat and leave until hot. Fry shredded mushrooms, a little at a time, until golden and done. Remove and drain. Continue frying until finished.
3. Arrange on a serving dish, scatter sesame seeds on top and garnish with vegetables before serving.

(Serves 2)

The angel mushroom belongs to the oyster mushroom family. It has a soft and juicy texture. Buy fresh mushrooms with a soft white color and no bruises. Beware not to add too much water to the dish as the mushroom will release its juice when cooked. Roast or leave to dry in the air before frying.

Omelet with Fresh Bean Curd Skin

(khai-jiaw fong-tao-hoo sod)

- 1 egg
- 1 cup fresh bean curd skin, chopped
- 1 teaspoon light soy sauce
- 1/2-1 teaspoon ground roasted dried hot chili
- 1 tablespoon black sesame seeds, roasted and seasoned
- 2 cups vegetable oil
- coriander leaves, shredded spring onion and red spur chili slices for garnish

1. Lightly beaten the egg, add fresh bean curd skin and season with light soy sauce, ground chili and sesame seeds. Stir to combine.
2. Pre-heat a pan of oil over medium heat until hot. Softly pour half of the egg mixture into the pan. With a spatula, spoon the oil over the egg and reduce to low heat. When the omelet becomes golden on one side, turn and cook until the other side is also golden and crispy. Remove and drain. Repeat the same process with the remaining half.
3. Arrange the omelet on a serving platter or, alternatively, top on hot steamed rice. Garnish with coriander leaves, spring onion and red spur chili. It goes well with hot chili sauce.

(Serves 2)

100 grams of fresh bean curd skin contains 47 grams of protein, 245 mg. of calcium, 494 mg. of phosphorous and 9.5 mg. of iron. It provides more nutritional value than other soybean products such as soybean milk and several kinds of tofu.

Spicy Corn Patties

(thod-mun khao-phod)

2 cups corn kernels, thinly sliced
1 1/2 cups oyster mushrooms, torn
3 tablespoons *kaeng khua* curry paste (page 130)
1 egg, lightly beaten
3 tablespoons rice flour
3 tablespoons tempura flour
1/2 teaspoon sea salt
3 cups vegetable oil
banana leaves for lining
Fresh vegetables: red lettuce leaves, green ork leaves

Dipping sauce

1/4 cup water
1/4 cup+2 tablespoons sugar
1/2 teaspoon sea salt
1/4 cup vinegar
1 red spur chili, seeded and pounded
1 cucumber, thinly sliced
2 tablespoons ground roasted peanut

1. To prepare the dipping sauce: Combine water, sugar, salt, vinegar and red spur chili in a sauce pot. Place over low heat and boil until it is slightly thickened. Remove from the heat and allow to cool. Pour over cucumber and roasted peanut just before serving.
2. Lightly pound corn kernels, oyster mushrooms and *kaeng khua* curry paste together. Transfer to a mixing bowl and add in egg. Stir to combine. Add rice flour, tempura flour and salt, stirring again. Put aside.
3. Place a pan with oil over medium heat until the oil is hot. With a spoon, scoop the corn mixture and shape to form a patty. Deep-fry in hot oil until golden and cooked through. Remove and drain off excess oil. Continue until the mixture is used up.
4. Arrange corn patties attractively on a bed of banana leaves, serve with the dipping sauce and fresh vegetables.

(Makes 25-30 pieces)

Spicy corn patties are cleverly created by mixing sweet corn kernels with small amount of red curry paste to add hot and spicy taste to the dish. Furthermore egg is added to give fluffy texture while rice flour and tempura flour are added to help combine the mixture.

Fried Tofu with Sweet Tamarind Sauce

(tao-hoo thod raad sauce ma-khaam-piak)

- 2 pieces (150 grams each) semi-hard white tofu
- 3 tablespoons vegetable oil
- 2 tablespoons shallot, chopped
- 3 tablespoons palm sugar
- 2 tablespoons light soy sauce
- 1/2 cup tamarind juice
- 2 tablespoons water or vegetable stock
- 1 tablespoon crisp-fried sliced garlic
- 2 tablespoons crisp-fried sliced shallot
- 7 fried dried hot chilies
- coriander leaves and red spur chili strips for garnish

1. Bring a pot of water (with small amount of salt) over high heat. Add in tofu and boil until done and floated to the surface. (The tofu will have a firm and chewy texture.) Remove and cut into cubes. Fry cooked tofu with small amount of oil over medium heat until golden on all sides. Put aside.
2. To prepare sweet tamarind sauce: Place a pan with oil over medium heat and leave until the oil is hot. Fry chopped shallot until golden and fragrant. Add palm sugar, light soy sauce, tamarind juice and water or stock. Stir and cook until the sauce is slightly thickened with a perfect balance of sour, sweet and salty. Turn off the heat.
3. Arrange fried tofu in a serving dish, spoon sweet tamarind sauce over and top with crisp-fried garlic, crisp-fried shallot and fried dried hot chilies. Garnish with coriander leaves and spur chili strips, serve at once.

(Serves 2)

The tamarind sauce should be cook to the right thickness that it nicely coats the tofu. Add sliced shallot and sliced garlic into the oil at a room temperature and start frying until they are completely crisp and a nice golden color is obtained.

Savory Fried Tempeh

(tempeh thod song-kreung)

- 1 pack (150 grams) fresh tempeh
- 10 cloves Thai garlic, peeled and sliced
- 3 shallots, sliced
- 1/2 teaspoon black pepper
- 1 tablespoon light soy sauce
- 2 teaspoons brown sugar
- 2 tablespoons tamarind juice
- 1/2 teaspoon sea salt
- 2 cups vegetable oil
- 1/4 cup crisp-fried shallot
- lettuce leaves and carrot slices for garnish

1. Cut tempeh into pieces and put aside.
2. Pound garlic, shallots and pepper together well. Add light soy sauce, sugar, tamarind juice and salt. Stir until completely dissolved. Transfer to a mixing bowl and toss with tempeh slices. Marinate at a room temperature for 10-15 minutes.
3. Place a wok of oil over medium-low heat until the oil is hot. Fry marinated tempeh until golden brown. Remove and drain. Continue frying until all the tempeh is used up.
4. Arrange on a serving dish and sprinkle crisp-fried shallot over the top. Garnish with lettuce leaves and carrot slices, serve at once.

(Serves 2-3)

Tempeh is made from soybean fermented with the mold named "Rhizopus oligosporus". It is one of Indonesian ethnic food. There are 2 types of tempeh sold in the market: steamed tempeh (usually called "fresh tempeh") and fried tempeh. Its fragrance is similar to fresh mushroom and can be cooked in many styles.

Stir-Fried Chilies with Snow Peas

(phrik-noom phad kub thua-khaek)

- 2 cups+2 tablespoons vegetable oil
- 21 pods snow pea, removed tough fibers from both sides
- 9 *noom* chilies with stems on
- 2 tablespoons large clove garlic, coarsely chopped
- 2 slices (1" long) mature ginger with skin-on, washed and bruised
- 1 1/2 tablespoons light soy sauce
- 1/4 teaspoon sea salt

1. Place a pan over medium heat and add 2 cups of oil. When the oil is very hot, fry snow pea for 1 minute until done and tender. Remove from the pan and put aside. Add small amount of oil into the pan, fry chilies for 1 minute until the skin is slightly brown and the flesh is tender. Remove and drain.
2. Add the remaining oil into the same pan and place over high heat. Sauté garlic and ginger until fragrant and golden. Add fried chilies and snow pea, stir to combine. Season with light soy sauce and salt, stirring and turn off the heat.
3. Dip out into a serving dish and serve at once. (Serves 2)

Noom chili is popularly used in the Northern region of Thailand. It has a long tapering fruit with a mildly hot taste and a green or light green to yellowish green color depending on the cultivated area. Buy those with fresh skin and firm stalks intact. A quick-fried method is used to maintain its sweet and juicy flesh.

Steamed Mushroom Curry

(haw-mok hed)

- 1/2 cup coconut cream
- 1/4 cup+2 tablespoons *kaeng khua* curry paste (page 130)
- 1 cup textured vegetable protein (TVP), soaked and chopped
- 1 tablespoon rice flour
- 1 duck or chicken egg
- 100 grams straw mushrooms, thinly sliced
- 100 grams angel mushrooms, torn
- 2 tablespoons kaffir lime leaves, shredded
- 1 1/2 tablespoons light soy sauce
- 1/2 cup sweet basil leaves, blanched and squeeze to dry
- 1/2 cup Indian mulberry leaves, blanched and squeeze to dry
- cooked coconut cream for topping
- shredded kaffir lime leaves, sliced red spur chili and coriander leaves for garnish
- small bowls or heat-proof ramekins for steaming

1. In a mixing bowl, stir coconut cream and *kaeng khua* curry paste together well. Add TVP and stir for 10 minutes until it absorbs some of the sauce. Add rice flour and egg, stir well. Add straw mushrooms, angel mushrooms and kaffir lime leaves. Stir until thickened. Season with light soy sauce and stir well.
2. Line blanched sweet basil leaves or Indian mulberry leaves at the base of each bowl, spoon the TVP mixture into the bowl until almost full. Arrange in a steamer and steam over boiling water for 10 minutes, using high heat. Remove the steamer from the heat, open the cover. Top each bowl with cooked coconut cream, sprinkle shredded kaffir lime leaves and red spur chili over and put on the cover. Return to the heat and steam for 1 more minute. Turn off the heat.
3. Arrange steamed curried mushrooms on a serving dish and garnish with coriander leaves before serving.

(Serves 8)

The mixture should be stirred continuously until the liquid reduces and is thickened. Blanch the sweet basil and Indian mulberry leaves and squeeze to dry before lining them at the base of each bowl. Use only young leaves as they are tender and have less bitter taste.

Steamed Egg Custard with Assorted Mushrooms

(khai toon hed ruam-mid)

- 2 eggs
- 1/4 cup semi-hard white tofu, boiled and mashed
- 1 cup water or vegetable stock (version 1 page 13)
- 1 1/2 tablespoons light soy sauce
- 1/4 teaspoon pepper
- 1/4 teaspoon sea salt
- 4 fresh small shiitake mushrooms, quartered
- 1/4 cup black ear mushrooms, sliced into strips
- 2 small straw mushrooms, thinly sliced
- 1 tablespoon shallot, thinly sliced
- 1 spring onion, sliced
- crisp-fried garlic and sliced spring onion for topping

1. In a bowl, break in eggs and beat lightly. Add tofu, water or vegetable stock, light soy sauce, pepper and salt. Stirring to combine. Add mushrooms, shallot and spring onion. Stir well. Divide among 3 cups and steam over hot boiling water for 8-10 minutes, using medium heat. When done, turn off the heat.
2. Remove from the steamer, sprinkle crisp-fried garlic and spring onion over the top and serve hot.

(Serves 3)

Thai egg custard with assorted mushrooms, tofu and sliced shallot. Choose small shallots with reddish purple skin; the flesh will be juicy sweet, soak them in cold water before peeling and slicing so your eyes will not be irritated.

Braised Tofu with Herbs

(tao-hoo-khaeng ob sa-moon-phrai)

- 3 pieces (230 grams each) hard white tofu
- 2 cups+2 tablespoons vegetable oil
- 3 coriander roots, sliced
- 2 teaspoons roasted coriander seeds
- 2 tablespoons palm sugar
- 1 tablespoon unbleached sugar
- 1 1/2 tablespoons sweet dark soy sauce
- 2 stems lemongrass, cut into 2" sections and bruised
- 1 piece (2" long) mature galangal, bruised
- 2 sticks (2" long) cinnamon
- 2 teaspoons cracked peppercorn
- 1/2 cup coconut cream
- 1/2 cup coconut milk
- 2 tablespoons tamarind juice
- 1/2 tablespoon sea salt
- 2 tablespoons seasoning sauce
- 1 tablespoon light soy sauce
- 5 kaffir lime leaves
- kaffir lime leaves and diagonally sliced red spur chili for garnish

1. In a pot of water, add small amount of salt and bring to the boil over high heat. Boil tofu until done and floated to the surface. Remove and put aside.
2. Put 2 cups of oil in a pan and place over medium heat until the oil is hot. Fry boiled tofu until golden, remove and drain. Diagonally cut into thin slices and put aside.
3. Pound coriander roots and seeds to a fine paste. Sauté in the same pan over low heat until fragrant. Add both kinds of sugar and sweet dark soy sauce. Continue cooking until fragrant, add lemongrass, galangal, cinnamon and peppercorn. Stirring, pour in coconut cream and coconut milk. Season with tamarind juice, salt, seasoning sauce and light soy sauce. Stir to mix well. Add fried tofu, tear kaffir lime leaves and put in. Stirring to combine and cover. Simmer for 30 minutes or until the tofu absorbs most of the sauce. Turn off the heat.
4. Transfer to a serving dish, garnish with kaffir lime leaves and red spur chili before serving.

(Serves 4)

Lemongrass and galangal provide unique flavor and fragrance to the dish. They are both beneficial to the digestive system. Select fresh lemongrass with plump and slightly red stems and mature galangal with brown skin.

Traditional Braised TVP

(neu protein ob sood dung-derm)

100 grams large-sized textured vegetable protein (TVP)
3 coriander roots
1/2 tablespoon black peppercorn
2 tablespoons mature ginger, cut into small pieces
1 cup coconut milk
2 teaspoons five Chinese spices powder
1 tablespoon palm sugar
1 tablespoon unbleached sugar
1 tablespoon seasoning sauce
2 tablespoons light soy sauce
2 teaspoons sweet dark soy sauce
Fresh vegetables: lettuce and coriander leaves
Boiled vegetables: carrot and potato, cut into pieces

1. Bring a pot of water to the boil over moderate heat. Add TVP and boil until tender. Remove, wash under cold water and squeeze to dry. Put aside.
2. In a mortar, pound coriander roots finely. Add black peppercorn and ginger, pound to a fine paste and put aside.
3. Put 1/2 cup of coconut milk into a pan, bring to a boil over moderate heat. Sauté the pounded mixture until fragrant, add five Chinese spices powder and stir to mix well. Season to taste with both sugar, seasoning sauce, light soy sauce and sweet dark soy sauce then add the remaining coconut milk. Put in TVP and toss to coat. Reduce to low heat, cover. Simmer until the sauce reduces and TVP absorbs most of the sauce (stir occasionally to prevent from getting burnt). Turn off the heat.
4. Dip out into a serving dish and attractively arrange assorted vegetables on the side.

(Serves 4)

Five Chinese spices powder consist of several spices, mainly are cinnamon, star anise, coriander seed, cumin and Szechwan peppercorn. All are ground and mixed together. Buy freshly mixed powder with strong aroma and store in a closed container. It can be kept at a room temperature or refrigerated for months.

Salty Tofu

(tao-hoo khem)

- 2 pieces (200 grams each) semi-hard white tofu
- 3 cups vegetable oil
- 1/2 cup water
- 1 tablespoon seasoning sauce
- 1 tablespoon light soy sauce
- 1 teaspoon unbleached sugar
- 1/2 teaspoon pepper
- small amount of white sesame seeds for topping
- coriander leaves for garnish
- Condiments: fresh lettuce leaves, coriander, boiled chopped carrot and boiled chopped potato

1. Add small amount of salt in a pot of water and bring to the boil over high heat. Boil tofu until done and floated to the surface. Remove and wash under running cold water, drain. Cut each piece to obtain 4 triangular slices and divide each slice into halves. Put aside.
2. Pre-heat a wok of oil over moderate heat. Fry tofu until golden on all sides. Remove and drain.
3. In another pan, pour in water and bring to the boil over moderate heat. Season with seasoning sauce, light soy sauce, sugar and pepper. Stirring, add fried tofu and put the cover on. Continue cooking until the sauce runs out. Turn off the heat.
4. Transfer to a serving dish, sprinkle sesame seeds over the top and garnish with coriander. Serve hot with condiments.

(Serves 3-4)

Semi-hard white tofu has a firm and chewy texture after boiling. It will not stick to the pan when fried and maintain its shape even when being cooked in the sauce for long hours.

Steamed Tofu and Mushrooms in Soy Sauce

(tao-hoo kub hed nueng see-ew)

- 2 pieces (250 grams each) soft white tofu
- 4 fresh shiitake mushrooms, score the caps lightly
- 20 grams black shiimeji mushrooms
- 2 eryngii mushrooms
- 20 grams enoki mushrooms
- Chinese celery leaves and stalks, red spur chili strips

The sauce

- 1 tablespoon chopped garlic
- 1/4 teaspoon cracked black pepper
- 1/4 cup vegetable stock (version 1 page 13)
- 1/2 teaspoon unbleached sugar
- 1 tablespoon light soy sauce
- 1 teaspoon seasoning sauce
- 1/4 teaspoon dark soy sauce
- 1 teaspoon olive oil
- 1/2 teaspoon Chinese rice wine

1. Bring a pot of water to the boil over high heat (add a dash of salt into water). Add tofu and boil until cooked through and floated to the surface (to obtain a chewy texture). Remove and put aside.
2. To prepare the sauce: Combine all ingredients together and put aside.
3. Cut (but not separate) the tofu to obtain 1/2 -1" cubes and arrange on a plate. Top with all mushrooms and spoon the sauce over. Place in a steamer and steam over high heat for 5 minutes or until the mushrooms are done. Remove from the heat.
4. Garnish with Chinese celery and red spur chili, best when serve hot.

(Serves 2)

It is recommended to boil tofu before used in order to reduce the nutty odor and to obtain a firm and chewy texture. Lightly cut the tofu so that it absorbs the sauce well enough. Select only freshly-made creamy white tofu for this recipe.

Braised Shiitake Mushrooms in Soy Sauce

(hed hom ob see-ew)

250 grams shiitake mushrooms
4 cups vegetable oil
1 teaspoon light soy sauce
1 teaspoon seasoning sauce
1 teaspoon pepper
coriander leaves for garnish
green ork leaves, cucumber and sliced tomato

1. With a towel, clean the mushrooms thoroughly. Trim away hard stalks and put aside. Preheat the oil in a pan over medium. Fry mushrooms for 3-4 minutes, remove and drain.
2. Drain off the oil and leave about 1 tablespoon in the frying pan. Return fried mushrooms to the pan, toss with light soy sauce, seasoning sauce and half of pepper. Add small amount of water and stir well. Put a cover on for a few minutes to let the mushrooms absorb the seasoning. Sprinkle the remaining pepper and turn off the heat.
3. Transfer to a serving dish and garnish with coriander leaves. Serve with green ork leaves, cucumber and tomato.

(Serves 2-3)

Select only those large-sized fresh shiitake mushrooms with thick flesh and no bruise is shown. Do not wash them but clean them softly with tea towel. Fry in the very hot oil until done before adding to the dish. Cook them quickly in order to maintain their juicy sweet flesh.

Phad Thai with Mung Bean Noodles

(phad thai wun-sen)

- 3 1/2 tablespoons vegetable oil
- 1 tablespoon shallot, chopped
- 1 tablespoon salted preserved Chinese radish, chopped
- 1 teaspoon chili powder
- 1/4 cup hard white tofu, cut into small pieces
- 3 seasoned shiitake mushrooms, cut into strips
- 1 pack (100 grams) dried mung bean noodles, soaked and cut into 4" sections
- 1/2 cup water
- 1/4 cup+1 tablespoon light soy sauce
- 1/4 cup+2 teaspoons unbleached sugar
- 1/4 cup tamarind juice
- 1 egg
- 1 cup bean sprouts
- 3 Chinese chives, cut into 1 1/2" sections
- 2 tablespoons ground roasted peanut
- omelette for garnish
- Fresh vegetables: shredded green mango, Chinese chives, lime wedges, banana blossom, bean sprouts etc.

Seasoned shiitake mushrooms

- 3 dried shiitake mushrooms, soaked until tender, trimmed away hard stalks and cut into strips
- 2 tablespoons vegetable oil
- 1 slice (1") mature ginger, bruised
- 2 spring onions, cut into 1 1/2" sections
- 1 cup liquid reserved from soaking shiitake mushrooms
- 1 1/2 tablespoons light soy sauce
- 1 teaspoon unbleached sugar

1. To prepare seasoned shiitake mushrooms: Fry the mushrooms in oil over medium heat until fragrant. Add ginger and spring onions, toss to combine. Add liquid reserved from soaking shiitake mushrooms. Season with light soy sauce and sugar. Reduce to low heat, simmer until the mushrooms absorb the sauce, remove and put aside.
2. Preheat a pan over medium heat. When it is hot, add in 3 tablespoons of oil. Add chopped shallot and fry until fragrant. Add preserved Chinese radish, chili powder, tofu and seasoned mushrooms. Cook until done, add mung bean noodles and water. Toss and cook until mung bean noodles are done. Season to taste with light soy sauce, sugar and tamarind juice, toss to mix well. With a spatula, remove the noodles to the side of the pan and add the remaining oil. Break in an egg, stir and cook until it is almost set. Fold the noodles over then add Chinese chives and bean sprouts. Stir-fry and toss to combine, turn off the heat.
3. Dip out into a serving dish, sprinkle roasted peanut over the top and garnish with omelette. Best when served with fresh vegetables.

(Serves 2)

Phad Thai Extra

(phad-thai song-kreung)

- 5 dried red spur chilies, seeded and soaked until tender
- 1¼ teaspoons sea salt
- 4 shallots, sliced
- 1 cup coconut cream
- ½ piece (65 grams) hard white tofu, diced and fried until lightly golden
- ¼ cup+1 tablespoon tamarind juice
- 2½ tablespoons palm sugar
- 1 (50 grams) salted preserved Chinese radish, wash and thinly sliced crosswise
- 250 grams small brown rice noodles
- ½ cup water
- ½ cup fresh bean sprouts, rooted
- 5 Chinese chives, cut into 1½" long
- 2 tablespoons roasted peanut, lightly crushed
- 1 lime, cut into wedges

  Fresh vegetables: banana blossom, Indian pennywort leaves, Chinese chives, bean sprouts, etc.

1. In a mortar, pound dried chili with ¼ teaspoon of salt thoroughly. Add shallots and pound to a smooth paste.
2. Place a pan with ½ cup of coconut cream over medium heat, cook until boiling and oil surfaces. Sauté pounded chili until fragrant and red oil surfaces. Add fried tofu, season with tamarind juice, palm sugar and the remaining salt. Taste for a balance of sour, salty and sweet. Add the remaining coconut cream, followed by salted preserved Chinese radish. Toss to combine well. (Reserve 2 tablespoons of the tofu mixture for topping). Add rice noodles and water, toss and cook until the noodles are done and tender. Add in bean sprouts and Chinese chives, toss lightly and turn off the heat.
3. Transfer to a serving plate and top with the reserved tofu. Arrange lime wedges and roasted peanut on the sides together with fresh vegetables. Enjoy while hot.

(Serves 2)

Freshly squeezed coconut cream is used in this recipe. It helps the noodles cook tenderly and aromatically. Stir occasionally to prevent the coconut cream from burning. Do not over-stir as its oil will take longer time to surface. This coconut oil is preferably used to sauté pounded chili paste instead of using the simple vegetable oil because it provides tempting aroma and nice red oil.

Fried Rice with Tri-Color Vegetables

(khao phad phak saam see)

- 2 tablespoons vegetable oil
- 1 tablespoon garlic, chopped
- 1/4 cup onion, diced
- 1/2 cup boiled carrot, diced
- 1/2 cup boiled corn kernels
- 2 cups cooked brown rice
- 1 tomato, diced
- 1 tablespoon light soy sauce
- 1/2 teaspoon sugar
- 1/8 teaspoon black pepper
- 1 tablespoon roasted white sesame seeds, coarsely ground
- coriander leaves for garnish

1. Preheat a pan of oil over medium heat. Fry chopped garlic until fragrant and golden. Add onion and fry until done and clear. Add carrot and corn kernels, toss to combine. Add cooked rice and tomato, toss again. Season to taste with light soy sauce, sugar and pepper. Toss well and remove from the heat.
2. Dip out into a serving dish, sprinkle white sesame seeds over the top and garnish with coriander leaves. Serve hot.

(Serves 2)

This recipe is easy to prepare as it has only a few ingredients. Brown rice used in this recipe is called *"mun poo"* rice which is one of the Thai rice species. Its crunchy texture is suit for fried rice. Carrot, corn kernels and tomato are added to make the dish looks colorful. Remember to add tomato at the last minute so that it will not become soggy.

Rice Seasoned with Vegetarian Shrimp Paste

(khao klook ka-pi je)

- 100 grams hard white tofu, mashed
- 2 teaspoons light soy sauce
- 1 cup vegetable oil
- 1 tablespoon garlic, chopped
- 1 tablespoon fermented tofu, finely mashed
- 1 tablespoon pickled Chinese olive, finely mashed (used instead of shrimp paste)
- 1 tablespoon water
- 1 teaspoon sugar
- 2 1/2 cups cooked brown rice
- 1 egg, lightly beaten
- 1/4 cup green mango, shredded
- 3 tablespoons shallot, sliced
- coriander leaves and hot chili slices for garnish
- Fresh vegetables: lime wedges and spring onion

Sweet tofu

- 1 tablespoon shallot, chopped
- 2 tablespoons vegetable oil
- 1 cup hard white tofu, diced and fried until golden
- 1 tablespoon light soy sauce
- 1 teaspoon sweet dark soy sauce
- 2 tablespoons palm sugar
- 1/4 cup water

1. To prepare sweet tofu: Fry shallot in oil over medium heat until golden and fragrant. Add tofu and toss well. Add light soy sauce, sweet dark soy sauce and palm sugar, toss to coat. Add in water and cook until the sauce reduces and the tofu becomes shiny.
2. To prepare seasoned fried tofu: Toss tofu and light soy sauce together. Fry tofu in hot oil over high heat for a few minutes. Reduce to medium heat and cook until no bubble remains and the tofu is golden crispy. Remove and drain.
3. Drain away the oil in the frying pan and leave only 3 tablespoons in the pan. Fry chopped garlic over medium heat until golden and fragrant. Combine fermented tofu, pickled Chinese olive and water together and add into the pan. Stir to combine and add sugar. Reduce to low heat, add cooked rice and toss well. Dip out into a bowl.
4. In another pan, add in 1 tablespoon of oil and place over low heat. Swirl the pan to coat, pour beaten egg and swirl to form a thin round sheet. When it is done, remove from the pan. Roll the omelette and cut across into thin strips.
5. Ladle shrimp paste rice onto a serving dish, arrange omelette strips, sweet tofu, seasoned fried tofu, green mango, and sliced shallot on the sides. Garnish with coriander leaves and hot chili. Serve with fresh vegetables.

(Serves 2)

This tasty dish can not be served without its scrumptious condiments. They are shredded green mango, shredded omelette, freshly sliced shallot and sweet tofu. Fry the tofu to obtain a chewy texture before cooking in a mixture of soy sauce and sugar.

Fried Rice with Red Fermented Tofu

(khao phad tao-hoo yee)

- 1 piece semi-hard white tofu (140 grams)
- 1 cup vegetable oil
- 1 tablespoon Thai garlic, pounded
- 3 tablespoons olive oil
- 1 tablespoon red fermented tofu, mashed finely
- 2 cups steamed brown rice
- 1 egg
- 1/2 teaspoon unbleached sugar
- 1 tablespoon+2 teaspoons liquid reserved from red fermented tofu
- 2 tablespoons sliced shallot
- hot chili and coriander leaves for garnish
- Condiments: sliced shallot, shredded green mango, lime wedge and sliced cucumber

1. Bring a pot of water (with a dash of salt) to the boil over medium heat. Add in tofu and cook until done and floated to the surface. Transfer to soak in water until cold. Remove and pat-dry, cut to obtain small dices. Fry in hot oil over medium heat until just golden. Drain on absorbent paper and put aside.
2. Fry garlic with 2 tablespoons of olive oil over medium heat until lightly golden. Remove only fried garlic and put aside. In the same pan, add in red fermented tofu and stir-fry until it smells fragrant. Add steamed rice, toss to coat well. Remove the rice to the side of the pan and add the remaining olive oil. Break in an egg, stir and cook until done. Toss the egg with cooked rice. Season to taste with sugar and liquid reserved from red fermented tofu. Toss to mix well. Add fried garlic, toss again and turn off the heat. Transfer fried rice to a mixing bowl and toss with sliced shallot.
3. Spoon fried rice onto a serving dish, garnish with hot chili and coriander. Enjoy with the condiments.

(Serves 2)

Finely mash red fermented tofu before tossing with cooked rice. Liquid reserved from the red fermented tofu is also used to add flavor and color to the dish. Condiments with a sour taste like green mango and lime are perfect choices that compliment the rich taste of this fried rice.

Stir-Fried Rice Noodles with Vegetables and Sweet Dark Soy Sauce

(phad see-ew)

- 1/2 piece (100 grams) hard white tofu
- 2 cups vegetable oil
- 2 kales, large-sized
- 250 grams flat rice noodles
- 1/2 tablespoon chopped garlic
- 2 bulbs pickled garlic, thinly sliced
- 2 tablespoons mashed yellow fermented tofu with its liquid
- 1 tablespoon dark fermented soybean
- 1/4 teaspoon sweet dark soy sauce
- 1 teaspoon unbleached sugar
- 100 grams cauliflower, cut into florets
- blanched kale tip for garnish

1. Coarsely mash hard tofu and leave to dry slightly. Fry in hot oil over medium heat until golden and crispy. Remove and drain on absorbent paper.
2. Wash the kales, discard tough green skin and diagonally slice the stems. Cut the leaves into 1" pieces and put aside.
3. Separate rice noodles evenly and put aside.
4. Drain off the oil in the frying pan and leave only 2 tablespoons, place the pan over medium heat until the oil is hot. Sauté chopped garlic until fragrant, add pickled garlic, fermented tofu and dark fermented soybean, followed with rice noodles. Stir-fry and toss to combine. Season with sweet dark soy sauce and sugar. Add in kales and cauliflower. Cook until everything is done, turn off the heat.
5. Transfer to a serving dish, sprinkle fried tofu on top and garnish with blanched kale tip. Serve at once.

(Serves 1)

Kale provides high beta-carotene which can prevent cancer. It also contains vitamin C, minerals and is high in calcium which can prevent coronary thrombosis and osteoporosis. Buy large-sized kale with plump stems, discard old leaves and peel away tough skin. Wash and lightly bruise the stems, then diagonally cut into slices.

Rice Noodle Rolls Thick Soup

(kuay-jub nam khon)

- 3 pieces (80-90 grams each) vegetarian pig intestine
- 1/2 cup unbleached sugar
- 8 cups water
- 2 star anises
- 1 stick (2" long) cinnamon
- 1 tablespoon five Chinese spices powder
- 2 teaspoons black peppercorns, cracked
- 3 bulbs pickled garlic
- 5 coriander roots, bruised
- 1 slice (2" long) mature galangal, bruised
- 3 1/2 tablespoons light soy sauce
- 3 tablespoons seasoning sauce
- 1 teaspoon sweet dark soy sauce
- 1/2 tablespoon palm sugar
- 1 tablespoon sea salt
- 5 (10-15 grams each) fresh shiitake mushrooms
- 7 straw mushrooms, halved
- 100 grams angel mushrooms, torn
- 2 hard-boiled eggs
- 300 grams rice noodle rolls
- 1 1/2 cups water
- 1 tablespoon rice flour
- 2 tablespoons water
- 1/2 cup sweet textured vegetable protein (TVP) (page 17)
- 1 piece (120 grams) semi-hard white tofu, cut into pieces and fried
- 1/4 cup spring onion, sliced
- 1/4 cup coriander, sliced
- 1/4 cup saw-leaves coriander, sliced

Additional seasoning: minced yellow spur chili in vinegar

1. Wash vegetarian pig intestine; blanch in hot boiling water over high heat for a moment. Remove and drain.
2. Put sugar in a new pot and place over medium heat until it becomes dark-colored caramel. When it starts to bubble, pour in water and cook until well-blended and boiling. Add pig intestine, followed by star anises, cinnamon, five Chinese spices powder, peppercorns, pickled garlic, coriander roots and galangal. When the soup boils well, reduce the heat to low. Season with light soy sauce, seasoning sauce, sweet dark soy sauce, palm sugar, salt and simmer for an hour, then add all mushrooms and boiled eggs. Continue cooking until everything is cooked and tender. Turn off the heat. Remove the intestine and eggs. When they are cold, cut the intestine into bite-sized and cut the eggs into wedges. Put aside.
3. In another pot, pour in water and bring to the boil over high heat. Cook rice noodle rolls until done and tender. Remove and put aside. Place a new pot with 1 1/2 cups of water over medium heat, cook until boiling. Add in cooked rice noodle rolls and cook until it returns to boiling. Mix rice flour with 2 tablespoons of water and stir into the pot. Continue cooking and stirring until it is thickened and done, turn off the heat.
4. Spoon one portion of cooked rice noodle rolls into a serving bowl, arrange pig intestine, sweet TVP, fried tofu and boiled egg on top. Spoon generous amount of thick soup over, scatter spring onion, coriander and saw-leaves coriander. Serve hot with chili in vinegar.

(Serves 4-6)

Rice Noodle Rolls Clear Soup

(kuay-jub nam sai)

8 cups water
1 head (400 grams) Chinese radish, cut into pieces
3 coriander roots, bruised
1/2 teaspoon black peppercorns, cracked
1 (100 grams) onion, cut into wedges
1 (170 grams) red apple, peeled and cut into pieces
2 tablespoons golden raisin
8 savory shiitake mushrooms (version 2 page 16)
2 tablespoons light soy sauce
1 tablespoon seasoning sauce
1/2 teaspoon sea salt
300 grams rice noodle rolls
1 1/2 cups water
1 tablespoon rice flour
2 tablespoons water
12 pieces seasoned vegetarian pig liver (page 230)
1/2 cup salty textured vegetable protein (TVP) (page 16)
1 piece (230 grams) hard white tofu, thinly sliced and fried
6 pieces crisp-fried dried bean curd skin
1/4 cup sliced spring onion
1/4 cup sliced coriander
coriander leaves for garnish
minced yellow spur chili in vinegar

1. To prepare the soup: Bring a pot of water to the boil over moderate heat. Add in Chinese radish, coriander roots, and peppercorns. When the soup boils, reduce the heat to low and simmer for 30 minutes. Add onion, apple and raisin, continue cooking for 10 minutes. Remove from the heat. Strain the stock into a new pot. Place the stock pot over medium heat and bring to the boil. Add savory shiitake mushrooms and cook until tender. When it returns to boiling, season with light soy sauce, seasoning sauce and salt. Stir to mix well, turn off the heat.
2. Bring a pot of water to the boil over high heat, add rice noodle rolls and boil until done. Remove and put aside. In a new pot, pour in 1 1/2 cups of water and bring to the boil over medium heat. Add in cooked rice noodle rolls and cook until boiling. Mix rice flour with 2 tablespoons of water and stir into the rice noodle pot. Stir continuously until thickened and done. Turn off the heat. (The batter can be omitted if preferred).
3. Spoon one portion of cooked rice noodle rolls into a serving bowl, arrange vegetarian pig liver, salty TVP, fried tofu and crisp-fired bean curd skin on top. Add generous amount of clear soup over and scatter spring onion and coriander over the top. Garnish with coriander leaves and serve immediately with chili in vinegar.

(Serves 4-6)

There are black and white peppercorns available in the market. Select large seeds with a natural light brown color if white peppercorn is used. It is recommended to roast the peppercorn before adding to the dish in order to obtain stronger aroma.

Rice Noodles with Vegetarian Brown Soup

(kuay-tiaw neu nam-tok je)

- 1 kilogram small brown rice noodles
- 1/4 cup skin-on Thai garlic, pounded and fried until crisp
- 8 cups vegetarian noodle stock (version 1 page 14 or version 3 page 15)
- 1 tablespoon ground pepper
- 1/2 cup Chinese celery, sliced
- 1/4 cup saw-leaves coriander, sliced
- 1/4 cup spring onion, sliced
- fresh bean sprouts and water morning glory
- Seasonings: light soy sauce, sugar and minced spur chili in vinegar

Vegetarian pig liver and lung

- 1 piece (200 grams) semi-hard white tofu, cut into triangular pieces
- 1 1/2 cups water
- 2 tablespoons pounded yellow fermented tofu
- 5 pieces large-sized textured vegetable protein (TVP), blanched and soaked until tender, squeezed and cut into pieces
- 1 1/2 tablespoons sweet dark soy sauce
- 2 star anises
- 1 stick (2" long) roasted cinnamon
- 2 teaspoons roasted coriander seed, ground
- 1 tablespoon seasoning sauce
- 1 tablespoon unbleached sugar

Braised veggi meat

- 5 pieces large-sized dark TVP
- 10 cubes yellow fermented tofu, pounded
- 1/3 cup water
- 1/2 cup dark fermented soybean with its liquid
- 1 tablespoon sweet dark soy sauce
- 1 teaspoon ground black pepper

1. To prepare vegetarian liver and lung: Bring a pot of water to the boil over high heat, add a pinch of salt and cook white tofu until done and floated to the surface. Remove and put aside. Place a pan over medium heat and pour in 1 1/2 cups of water. When it is hot, add fermented tofu, TVP, sweet dark soy sauce, star anises, cinnamon, ground coriander seed, seasoning sauce, sugar and stir to mix well. Add cooked tofu and lightly stir. Reduce to low heat and simmer until tofu is tender and the sauce reduces. Turn off the heat.
2. To prepare braised veggi meat: Bring a pot of water to the boil over medium heat, cook TVP until done and tender. Remove and wash under cold water. Squeeze to dry and put aside. Place a pan over medium heat, add in fermented tofu, water, dark fermented soybean, sweet dark soy sauce and black pepper. Stir to combine, add cooked TVP and turn the heat to low. Simmer until everything is tender and the sauce reduces. Turn off the heat. Cut braised TVP into slices and put aside.
3. Place a new pot of water over high heat and bring to the boil. Cook rice noodles, bean sprouts and water morning glory together in the hot boiling water until done. Dip out into a serving bowl, arrange vegetarian meat prepared in step 1 and 2 over the noodles. Sprinkle fried garlic on top and spoon generous amount of hot stock into the bowl. Add pepper, Chinese celery, saw-leaves coriander and spring onion. Serve hot with the seasonings.

(Serves 4-5)

Fried Rice Noodles with Mixed Vegetables and Gravy

(kuay-tiaw raad-naa)

- 3 tablespoons vegetable oil
- 1/2 teaspoon sweet dark soy sauce
- 250 grams flat brown or plain rice noodles
- 15 cloves chopped Thai garlic
- 2 bulbs pickled garlic, chopped
- 2 tablespoons dark fermented soybean
- 2 cubes yellow fermented tofu
- 2 large kales, peeled off tough green skin and cut into pieces
- 10 slices carrot, 1/2 cup cauliflower, cut into florets
- 3 ears baby corn, sliced diagonally
- 5 straw mushrooms, halved
- 5 fresh shiitake mushrooms
- 1/2 piece (65 grams) hard white tofu, thinly sliced and fried
- 2 cups vegetable stock (version 1 page 13)
- 1 tablespoon seasoning sauce
- 1 tablespoon light soy sauce
- 1/2 teaspoon sea salt
- 1 teaspoon palm sugar, 1 teaspoon brown sugar
- 1/2 tablespoon vinegar
- 1 tablespoon tapioca flour
- 1 tablespoon arrowroot flour
- 2 tablespoons water, 1/2 teaspoon pepper
- kale tips for garnish

Pickled chili in vinegar

- 10 green and red hot chilies
- 5 cloves Thai garlic, peeled
- 2 slices mature galangal
- 2 tablespoons fruit vinegar
- 1/2 tablespoon brown sugar
- 1 tablespoon lime juice
- 2 tablespoons vegetable stock (version 1 page 13)

1. To prepare pickled chili in vinegar: Dry-fry hot chilies, garlic and galangal over medium heat until fragrant and done. Transfer to a mortar and coarsely pound together. Dip out into a sauce bowl, season with vinegar, sugar, lime juice, stock and stir until sugar has completely dissolved.
2. Place a pan over high heat until very hot, add 1 tablespoon of oil, small amount of water (to soften the noodles) and sweet dark soy sauce. Add rice noodles, tossing and stirring until the noodles is fragrant and slightly brown. Remove from the heat and put aside.
3. To prepare the gravy: Combine garlic, pickled garlic, fermented soybean and fermented tofu together. Place a new pan over medium heat and add in the remaining oil. Sauté the mixture until fragrant, add kales, carrot, cauliflower, baby corn and cook until done. Add mushrooms and fried tofu, stir to mix well. Pour in stock and season with seasoning sauce, light soy sauce, salt, sugar and vinegar. When it boils, mix both flour with water and stir into the gravy. Stir continuously until thickened and done. Turn off the heat.
4. Arrange one portion of fried noodles on a serving dish, spoon the vegetables with some gravy over. Sprinkle on top with pepper and garnish with kale tips before serving.

(Serves 2-3)

Rice Noodles in Red Sauce

(kuay-tiaw yen-ta-fo haeng)

- 100 grams flat rice noodles
- 1/2 cup water morning glory, cut into 2" pieces
- 2 pieces vegetarian squid, cut into slices
- 2 pieces vegetarian preserved squid, cut into slices
- 3 (10 grams each) vegetarian shrimps
- 4 vegetarian fish balls
- 1/4 cup white jelly fungus, soak until tender and cut into pieces
- 1 savory shiitake mushroom, quartered (version 2 page 16)
- 1 tablespoon *yen ta fo* sauce
- 1 teaspoon hot sauce
- 1 teaspoon fried salted preserved Chinese radish
- 1 tablespoon Chinese celery, sliced
- 2 crisp-fried vegetarian wontons

Yen ta fo sauce (red sauce) (3/4 cup)

- 1 cube red fermented tofu, about 1 1/2" size
- 1/2 cup+1 tablespoon liquid from red fermented tofu
- 1/4 cup+1 tablespoon tomato ketchup
- 1/2 cup vegetable stock (version 1 page 13)
- 1/4 cup+1 tablespoon sugar
- 1 teaspoon vegetable oil

Hot sauce (3/4 cup)

- 1 tablespoon Thai chilies (16 pieces)
- 5 black peppercorns
- 1/2 cube red fermented tofu, about 1/2" size
- 1 tablespoon light soy sauce
- 1/2 teaspoon sugar
- 1/4 teaspoon sea salt
- 2 tablespoons lime juice

1. To prepare *yen ta fo* sauce: Finely pound or mash red fermented tofu and its liquid to a smooth paste. Dip out into a sauce bowl, add tomato ketchup, stock and sugar. Stir to mix well. Add in oil, stirring again. It should taste sweet and salty, put aside.
2. To prepare hot sauce: Pound hot chilies and peppercorns thoroughly. Add red fermented tofu and pound to a fine paste. Season with light soy sauce, sugar, salt and lime juice. Stir to dissolve and put aside.
3. Cook rice noodles and water morning glory in a pot of hot boiling water over high heat until done, remove and put into a serving dish. Cook vegetarian seafood and white jelly fungus in the same way and add to the rice noodles. Arrange savory shiitake mushroom on top. Spoon some *yen ta fo* sauce and hot sauce over, sprinkle on top with fried salted Chinese radish and sliced Chinese celery. Place crisp-fried wontons on the side and serve at once.

(Serves 1)

Yen ta fo sauce used in this recipe or stir-fried noodle is instant sauce sold in a bottle. The sauce is smoothly thick and reddish pink. Keep the sauce in a container with cover and put in a refrigerator.

Vegetarian Seafood Sukiyaki

(su-kee tha-lay je)

- 2 cups vegetable stock (version 1 page 13)
- 1/4 cup sukiyaki sauce
- 1 tablespoon light soy sauce
- 1/2 cup fresh *hookee*, cut into long strips
- 2 straw mushrooms, cut
- 2 fresh shiitake mushrooms
- 1/4 cup oyster mushrooms, torn
- 7 (50 grams) vegetarian shrimps
- 2 pieces vegetarian squid, cut into 1"x2" pieces
- 100 grams Chinese cabbage, cut into bite-sized
- 50 grams Chinese morning glory, cut into 2" pieces
- 1/2 cup enoki mushrooms
- 1/2 cup Chinese celery, cut into 1 1/2" pieces
- 1/2 cup mung bean noodles, soaked until tender and cut into short segments

Condiments: chopped hot chilies and lime wedges

red spur chili strips and Chinese celery sprig for garnish

Sukiyaki sauce (3/4-1 cup)

- 2 cubes red fermented tofu, about 1 1/2" size
- 2 tablespoons vegetable stock (version 1 page 13)
- 1/4 cup tomato ketchup
- 1 tablespoon sugar
- 1/4 cup vinegar
- 1 teaspoon sesame oil
- 1 tablespoon roasted white sesame seeds

1. To prepare sukiyaki sauce: Finely pound or mash red fermented tofu, add stock and tomato ketchup. Season with sugar, vinegar, sesame oil and stir to mix well. Add sesame seeds, put aside.
2. Bring a pot of vegetable stock to the boil over high heat. Add in sukiyaki sauce and light soy sauce. When it boils again, add *hookee* and stir. Add all mushrooms and cook until done. Add vegetarian shrimps and squid, followed by Chinese cabbage, Chinese morning glory, enoki mushrooms, Chinese celery and mung bean noodles. When everything is cooked through, turn off the heat.
3. Dip out into a serving bowl, garnish with red spur chili and Chinese celery sprig. Best when serve hot with sukiyaki sauce and condiments.

(Serves 1-2)

Sukiyaki sauce can be prepared and keep refrigerated many days in advance. Always store vegetarian meat, vegetarian seafood, tofu and all vegetables in your refrigerator for a handy use, then you can have this delicious dish whenever you like.

Wonton Soup

(kiaw nam)

- 1/2 pack (75 grams) wonton sheet, size 3"x3"
- 2 flowering cabbage cut into 1 1/2" long
- 4 garland chrysanthemum, cut away the earthen base
- 6 cups vegetable stock (version 2 page 13)
- oil from fried garlic
- Seasonings: pickled chili slices in vinegar, chili powder

The filling

- 1/2 teaspoon peppercorn
- 10 cloves Thai garlic, peeled
- 3 coriander roots, sliced
- 2 tablespoons vegetable oil
- 50 grams coarsely chopped abalone mushrooms
- 50 grams coarsely chopped straw mushrooms
- 1/3 cup steamed taro, finely mashed
- 1/3 cup steamed potato, finely mashed
- 1/3 cup boiled water chestnut, coarsely chopped
- 1 1/2 teaspoons seasoning sauce
- 1 1/2 teaspoons light soy sauce
- 2-3 tablespoons finely chopped carrot
- 1/4 cup dried shiitake mushrooms, soaked, squeezed and fried until lightly golden then chopped finely

1. To prepare the filling: Pound peppercorn to a powder, add garlic and coriander roots and pound to a fine mixture. Sauté the mixture in a pan of oil over medium heat until fragrant. Add abalone mushrooms, straw mushrooms and cook until done. Add taro, potato and water chestnut, stir-fry to combine. Season with seasoning sauce and light soy sauce. Add carrot and shiitake mushrooms, toss to combine and leave to cool.
2. Spread wonton sheet on a flat surface. Put 1 teaspoon of the filling onto the center and fold in half to form a triangle. Fold both pointed ends together, brush the edges with water and press to seal. Keep in a container and cover with damp cloth to prevent from dryness. Repeat the process until all wonton sheets are used up.
3. Bring a pot of water to the boil on medium heat, put in wontons and boil until cooked through and floated to the surface. Transfer to soak in a bowl of cold water for a few seconds. Remove and drain. Arrange cooked wontons among serving bowls and toss with oil from fried garlic. Cook flowering cabbage and garland chrysanthemum in the same pot, drain and add into the bowls. Spoon generous amount of hot stock over and serve immediately with seasonings.

(Serves 4)

The sweetness of vegetable stock comes from many fruits such as apple and raisin. Select fresh red apples with wrinkle-free skin and no rotten spots or bruises. Peel and immediately put into the stock pot to prevent from discoloration. Always use golden raisin as its firm flesh will not become mushy after cooked and the stock will have a nice golden color.

Vegetarian Chicken Rice

(khao-mun-kai je)

- 5 coriander roots
- 20 cloves Thai garlic, peeled
- 1 cup vegetable oil
- 40 grams mature ginger with skin, bruised
- 1 teaspoon black peppercorns, cracked
- 1 3/4 cups vegetable stock (version 1 page 13)
- 2 cups uncooked brown rice
- 1 tablespoon seasoning sauce
- 1/2 teaspoon sea salt
- 1 teaspoon unbleached sugar
- 6 straw mushrooms, thinly sliced
- 50 grams angel mushrooms, torn
- 60 grams abalone mushrooms, thinly sliced
- 1/2 cup hot water
- 300 grams fresh bean curd skin cake, cut into 0.5 cm slices
- cucumber slices
- coriander leaves for garnish

The sauce

- 1/4 cup dark fermented soybean, mashed finely
- 1 tablespoon palm sugar
- 2 tablespoons unbleached sugar
- 1/4 cup+2 tablespoons tamarind juice
- 2 tablespoons water
- 2 tablespoons chopped mature ginger
- 1 1/2 tablespoons chopped green and red hot chilies
- 1 tablespoon Thai garlic, peeled and chopped

1. Pound 3 coriander roots finely, add garlic and pound to a fine paste. Sauté with 2 tablespoons of oil on medium heat until fragrant. Add ginger and peppercorns, cook until fragrant. Add stock and stir to mix well. Bruise the remaining coriander roots and add in. Wash the rice and add to the pan. Toss to combine. Season with seasoning sauce, salt and sugar. When it boils, add all mushrooms, toss and cover. Reduce to medium-low heat and simmer for 8 minutes. Remove the cover, toss and stir the rice and add hot water. Turn to low heat and continue cooking for 5 minutes. Open and toss again. Put the cover on and cook until everything is done. Turn the heat to the lowest level and cook until the rice is completely done. Turn off the heat. Let it stand for a moment then open and stir lightly.
2. Place a pan with the remaining oil over medium heat and wait until the oil is hot, fry slices of bean curd skin until lightly golden. Remove and drain.
3. In a sauce pot, combine dark fermented soybean, palm sugar, sugar, tamarind juice and water together. Cook over low heat until boiling. Remove from the heat. Allow to cool, stir in chopped ginger, hot chilies and garlic.
4. Spoon cooked rice onto a serving dish, arrange fried bean curd skin and cucumber slices on the side. Garnish with coriander leaves and serve with the sauce.

(Serves 4)

Brown rice is obtained from manually milled rice grain. The process is very simple that the rice is put in a big wooden mortar and continuously pounded with a huge pestle until its shell is removed.

Vegetarian Rice Soup

(khao-tom mang-sa-wi-rad)

1 cup uncooked brown jasmine rice
1/4 cup uncooked glutinous rice
7 cups vegetable stock (version 1 page 13)
2 tablespoons light soy sauce
5 straw mushrooms, quartered
6 fresh shiitake mushrooms, discard stems
1 cup oyster mushrooms, torn
1/2 cup black ear mushrooms, cut into small pieces
100 grams vegetarian shrimps
1/2 cup hard white tofu, cut into thin slices and fry until slightly golden
2 teaspoons preserved Chinese cabbage
2 tablespoons fried garlic
1/4 cup sliced spring onion and coriander
pepper
Condiments: light soy sauce, sugar, pickled chili in vinegar and chili powder

1. Wash both kinds of rice and put into a pot. Add stock and place over medium heat. Stir frequently until boiling and the rice is done and tender. Season to taste with light soy sauce. Add all mushrooms and vegetarian shrimps, continue cooking until everything is cooked through. Turn off the heat and add fried tofu.
2. Ladle into a soup bowl, scatter on top with preserved Chinese cabbage, fried garlic, sliced spring onion, coriander and pepper. Serve hot with condiments.

(Serves 4)

Small amount of glutinous rice is added to thicken the soup. Select only fresh and plump mushrooms, the glutamic acid contained in these mushrooms gives this rice soup a fantastic flavor.

Vegetarian Congee

(joke je)

Portion for one serving

- 1½ cups boiled rice
- 2 tablespoons seasoned vegetarian minced pork
- 3-4 pieces seasoned vegetarian pig liver
- 1 savory shiitake mushroom (version 2 page 16)
- 2 teaspoons light soy sauce
- 1 tablespoon shredded young ginger
- 1 tablespoon sliced Chinese celery
- freshly ground pepper as required

Boiled rice

- 1 cup uncooked new jasmine rice
- ¼ cup uncooked new sticky rice
- 10 cups vegetable stock (version 3 page 14)
- 5 fragrant pandanus leaves, tied
- 1 teaspoon sea salt

Seasoned vegetarian minced pork

- 15 pieces textured vegetable protein (TVP) (1" in diameter)
- 3 tablespoonsvegetable oil
- ¼ cup stalks of dried shiitake mushrooms, soaked, squeezed to dry then bruised and chopped
- 1 tablespoon+1 teaspoon light soy sauce
- 1 teaspoon seasoning sauce
- ½ teaspoon palm sugar
- 2 tablespoons vegetable stock (version 3 page 14)
- freshly ground black pepper as required

Seasoned vegetarian pig liver

- 1 piece (250 grams) semi-hard white tofu
- 1 cup+2 tablespoons vegetable oil
- 2 cups vegetable stock (version 3 page 14)
- 1 tablespoon seasoning sauce
- 1½ teaspoons palm sugar
- ½ teaspoon freshly ground black pepper
- 1 tablespoon sweet dark soy sauce

1. To make boiled rice: Wash both kinds of rice, soak overnight or at least 3 hours. Wash again and blend coarsely with 1 cup of stock. Transfer to a pot and add the remaining stock, stirring well. Place the rice pot over medium heat, stir frequently. When it boils, put in pandanus leaves and continue cooking for 35 minutes or until the rice is done and thickened. Season with salt.
2. To make vegetarian minced pork: Bring a pot of water to the boil over medium heat, add (plain or dark) TVP and cook until done. Remove, wash under cold water and squeeze to dry, then chop finely. Place a pan with oil over medium heat. When the oil is hot, sauté shiitake stalks until fragrant. Add TVP and toss to combine. Season with light soy sauce, seasoning sauce, palm sugar, pepper and add stock. Cook until TVP is tender and absorb all the sauces.
3. To make vegetarian pig liver: Wash tofu and boil in a pot of hot water over medium heat until floated to the surface. Remove and allow to cool. Cut boiled tofu into thin triangular slices and fry in hot oil until slightly golden. Remove and put aside. Drain off the oil and leave only 2 tablespoons in the frying pan, add stock and season with seasoning sauce, sugar, pepper and sweet dark soy sauce. Stir well then return fried tofu back into the pan. Reduce the heat to low, simmer until the sauce reduces by half.
4. To serve: Heat boiled rice until hot, spoon one portion into a serving bowl. Top with vegetarian minced pork, pig liver and savory shiitake mushroom. Add light soy sauce, ginger, Chinese celery and pepper, serve hot.

(Serves 8)

Fermented Rice Vermicelli with Green Curry

(kha-nom-jeen kaeng khiaw waan)

- 1 cup *phak waan baan*, leaves only
- 1/4 cup coconut cream
- 4 1/2 cups coconut milk
- 200 grams straw mushrooms, quartered
- 50 grams abalone mushrooms, torn
- 100 grams oyster mushrooms, torn
- 3 tablespoons palm sugar
- 3 tablespoons light soy sauce
- 2 tablespoons seasoning sauce
- 3 teaspoons sea salt
- 100 grams vegetarian meatballs, blanched
- 5 Thai eggplants, quartered
- 50 grams pea eggplants
- 1 cup coconut shoot, cut into 1" cubes
- 1/2 cup shredded wild ginger
- 1 cup sweet basil leaves
- 1 cup coconut cream
- 2 kilograms fermented plain or brown rice vermicelli
- shredded wild ginger and red spur chili slices for garnish

Curry paste

- 200 grams green curry paste (page 19)
- 3 tablespoons coriander root, sliced
- 4 shallots, sliced
- 15 cloves Thai garlic, peeled and sliced
- 2 teaspoons roasted coriander seeds, ground
- 1 teaspoon roasted cumin, ground
- 2 cups coconut milk

1. To prepare the curry paste: combine green curry paste, coriander root, shallots, garlic, coriander seeds, cumin and coconut milk in a blender and blend to a smooth mixture.
2. Thoroughly blend *phak waan baan* leaves with coconut cream, strain and reserve only the green liquid.
3. Combine the curry paste with coconut milk in a pot and place over medium heat. Stir to combine and cook until boiling. Add all mushrooms and cook until done. Pour in the green liquid in step 2 to obtain the nice green curry sauce. Season to taste with palm sugar, light soy sauce, seasoning sauce and salt. Add blanched meatballs and both eggplants. When it boils again, add coconut shoot (Do not over-cooked as the shoot will be too tough). Add wild ginger and sweet basil leaves. When done, add coconut cream and turn off the heat.
4. Dip out into a serving bowl, garnish with wild ginger and spur chili slices. Serve with fermented rice vermicelli.

(Serves 6)

Fermented Rice Vermicelli with Chili Peanut Sauce

(kha-nom-jeen nam-phrik)

- 1 1/4 cups mung beans
- 4 cups water
- 7 straw mushrooms, chopped
- 50 grams angel mushrooms, chopped
- 1 1/2 tablespoons sea salt
- 3 cups coconut cream
- 150 grams palm sugar
- 150 grams unbleached sugar
- 1/2 cup tamarind juice
- 2 tablespoonslime juice
- 1 *som saa* juice (a kind of citrus with dark green rugged skin)
- 2 tablespoons a mixture of pounded fried dried red spur chilies and ginger
- 1/4 cup crisp-fried sliced shallot, broken into pieces
- 1/4 cup crisp-fried sliced garlic, broken into pieces
- 1/4 cup roasted peanuts, pounded
- 1 kilogram fermented plain or brown rice vermicelli
- fried dried hot chilies for garnish
- Condiments: sliced yard-long bean, blanched shredded water morning glory, assorted tempura flowers, etc.

1. Wash the mung beans, discard bad beans and dirt. Dry-fry in a pan over low heat until brown, turn off the heat. Transfer to a mortar and pound to remove the shells. Discard shells and reserve 1 cup of hulled mung beans.
2. Cook hulled mung beans in a pot of water over high heat until done and tender and the water runs dry. (Skim off bubbles and shells so that the beans will not turn dark). Remove from the heat and pound finely.
3. In another pot, cook straw mushrooms and angel mushrooms with 1 tablespoon of salt over medium heat until done (no water is required). Add coconut cream and bring back to the boil. Stir slowly in the same direction while cooking. Remove from the heat.
4. Combine cooked mushrooms and coconut cream with mung bean paste. Stir well. Season with the remaining salt, palm sugar, sugar, tamarind juice, lime juice and *som saa* juice. Taste for a balance of sweet, sour and salty. Add in pounded fried dried chilies and ginger mixture and stir to combine. Add fried shallot, fried garlic and roasted peanuts (reserve some of each for topping).
5. Arrange fermented rice vermicelli on a serving dish, spoon generous amount of the sauce over and top with fried dried hot chilies and the reserved fried shallot, fried garlic and roasted peanuts. Serve at once with condiments.

(Serves 4)

Fermented Rice Vermicelli with Banana Blossom Curry Sauce

(kha-nom-jeen nam-yaa hua-plee)

4 cups coconut cream
15 straw mushrooms, sliced and pounded
100 grams angel mushrooms, torn and pounded
2 tablespoons sea salt
1 tablespoon seasoning sauce
2 tablespoons palm sugar
1 head banana blossom, discarded purple outer leaves and reserved only white part
7 kaffir lime leaves
1 kilogram fermented plain or brown rice vermicelli
10 fried dried hot chilies
Condiments: sliced pickled mustard green, fresh bean sprouts, sliced yard-long bean and hairy basil leaves
hairy basil sprigs for garnish

Curry paste

100 grams red curry paste (page 18)
50 grams Southern red curry paste (page 18)
50 grams green curry paste (page 19)
5 shallots, sliced
17 cloves Thai garlic, peeled and sliced
1/2 teaspoon kaffir lime rind, finely sliced
3 wild ginger roots, sliced
1 cup coconut cream

1. To prepare curry paste: Combine all curry paste, shallots, garlic, kaffir lime rind, wild ginger and coconut cream in a blender and blend well.
2. Pour blended curry paste into a pot, add coconut cream and place over medium heat, stir and cook to boiling. Add pounded straw mushrooms and angel mushrooms and cook until done. Season with salt, seasoning sauce and palm sugar, stir well. When it returns to boiling, turn the heat up to high. Slice banana blossom directly into the sauce pot and press with a ladle to completely immerse in the liquid (this is to prevent from discoloration). When everything is done, tear kaffir lime leaves and add to the curry sauce. Turn off the heat.
3. Arrange fermented rice vermicelli on a serving dish, spoon generous amount of the curry sauce and banana blossom over. Garnish with hairy basil sprig and fried dried hot chilies, serve with condiments.

(Serves 6)

Banana blossom is part of the banana flowers hanging at the end of a clump of bananas and it will not grow to be the fruits. The most popular variety is "*nam waa*" banana as it tastes bitter less. Select fresh and heavy one with the bright reddish purple outer leaves, no sign of wrinkles or black marks.

Southern Rice Salad with Assorted Vegetables

(khao yum pak-tai mang-sa-wi-rad)

- 3 cups uncooked brown rice, 2 1/2 cups water
- 1/2 cup Indian mulberry leaves juice
- 2 tablespoons coconut cream, a pinch of sea salt
- Condiments: roasted grated coconut, shredded lemongrass, bean sprouts, shredded yard-long bean, shredded wild pepper leaves, shredded Indian pennywort leaves, shredded Indian mulberry leaves, thinly sliced stinky beans, shredded kaffir lime leaves, pomelo flesh, thinly sliced garcinia flesh, shredded green mango, roasted chili flake

Vegetarian "Budu" clear sauce

- 12 cups water, 5 stems lemongrass, cut into 1" sections and bruised
- 2 slices (1" long) mature galangal
- 10 shallots, bruised
- 15 cloves Thai garlic, peeled and bruised
- 1 kaffir lime, 5 kaffir lime leaves, torn
- 10 cubes yellow fermented tofu, mashed
- 3/4 cup dark fermented soybean
- 1/2 cup sweet dark soy sauce
- 300 grams palm sugar, 1/2 cup brown sugar
- 1/4 cup each seasoning sauce and light soy sauce

Vegetarian "Budu" thick sauce

- 5 stems lemongrass, cut into 1" sections
- 2 slices (1" long) mature galangal
- 10 shallots, 15 cloves Thai garlic, peeled
- 1 kaffir lime, 5 kaffir lime leaves, torn
- 10 cubes yellow fermented tofu, mashed
- 3/4 cup dark fermented soybean
- 12 cups water, 1/2 cup sweet dark soy sauce
- 300 grams palm sugar, 1/2 cup brown sugar
- 1/4 cup each seasoning sauce and light soy sauce

1. To prepare clear sauce: Place a pot of water over medium heat until boil. Add lemongrass, galangal, shallots, garlic, kaffir lime and its leaves. When it boils again, add the remaining ingredients and stir to mix well. Reduce to low heat and simmer until the sauce reduces by half. Allow to cool, strain and reserve the liquid.
2. To prepare thick sauce: Dry-fry lemongrass, galangal, shallots, garlic, kaffir lime and its leaves over medium heat until fragrant. Leave to cool then slice into small pieces. Peel off the cooked kaffir lime rind and slice into pieces. Put all sliced herbs except kaffir lime into a blender, add fermented tofu, fermented soybean and 2 cups of water. Blend to a smooth puree. Transfer to a pot, add the remaining ingredients, stir to combine. Place over medium heat, add in kaffir lime and cook until the sauce is slightly thickened.
3. Wash uncooked rice and drain. Bring a pot of water to the boil over medium heat, add in rice and salt. Stir well and cover, stir occasionally. When it is nearly cooked, add Indian mulberry leaves juice and coconut cream. Stir and cover. When the liquid almost dries out, tilt the pot to one side and continue cooking until it is completely dry. Stir to mix well. Remove from the heat, keep the cover on so that the rice is continuously cooking through.
4. Spoon the rice onto a serving platter, arrange small amount of each condiments and serve separately with both kinds of sauces.

(Serves 4)

www.sangdad.com